A-Z of ENGLISH

Ronald Ridout's
A-Z of ENGLISH

Illustrated by Tim Jaques
Designed by Neil Straker
Edited by Michael Tristram

GRANADA

Published by Granada Publishing 1985
Granada Publishing Ltd
8 Grafton Street, London W1X 3LA

British Library Cataloguing in Publication Data

Ridout, Ronald
Ronald Ridout's A–Z of English.
1. English language—Dictionaries, Juvenile
I. Title
423 PE1628.5

ISBN 0-246-12468-7 (hardback)
0-246-12707-4 (limp)

Printed and bound in Great Britain by
Hazell Watson & Viney, Aylesbury

INTRODUCTION

This is not just an ordinary grammar book. It is meant to help you make the most of the English language in every way.

Do you know how to write letters, invitations and stories? How many different kinds of joke, poem or word game do you know? Can you build new words with prefixes and suffixes? If you come across a strange word, do you know how to work out where it comes from, and what it means? Do you know when a sentence is not a sentence?

The better you know English, the more success and fun you will have using the language. This book will teach you the rules of the game of standard English, with plenty of interesting examples and problems to solve.

Ronald Ridout's *A–Z of English* is arranged in alphabetical order, to help you find what you're looking for, and there are lots of cross references*. An asterisk * after certain words means that you can look them up elsewhere in the book – the one above tells you that you can find out more about cross references under 'c'. So you can use this book as a reference book if you have a problem about English, or you can just dip in anywhere and read it. Either way, you're sure to learn something new!

abbreviations

An abbreviation is a shortened form of a word or words. Sometimes it is the first part of the word that makes the abbreviation, such as Capt for captain or Aug for August. Sometimes it is the first letter and the last, as in Rd for road or Dr for doctor. Sometimes it is just the initials of the words, eg NW for north-west or PTO for Please turn over.

It used to be necessary to put a full stop after an abbreviation to show it was an abbreviation, but this practice is gradually dying out. These, for example, rarely have a full stop today:

AD	Anno Domini (in the year of the Lord)	**ie**	id est (that is)
am	ante meridiem (before noon)	**IQ**	Intelligence Quotient
anon	anonymous	**kg**	kilogram(s)
approx	approximate	**kph**	kilometres per hour
arr	arrival or arrive(s)	**mod cons**	modern conveniences
Ave	Avenue	**mph**	miles per hour
BBC	British Broadcasting Corporation	**Mr**	Mister
BC	Before Christ	**Mrs**	Mistress
Bros	brothers	**NATO**	North Atlantic Treaty Organization
BSc	Bachelor of Science	**NB**	nota bene (note well)
cg	centigram(s)	**pm**	post meridiem (after noon)
cm	centimetre(s)	**pop**	population
Co	Company or County	**pp**	pages
Col	Colonel	**PR**	public relations
dep	departs	**pro**	professional
Dr	doctor	**rpm**	revolutions per minute
EEC	European Economic Community	**RSVP**	Répondez, s'il vous plaît (please reply)
eg	exempli gratia (for example)	**sae**	stamped addressed envelope
GB	Great Britain	**Sgt**	Sergeant
gm	gram(s)	**SW**	south-west
h&c	hot and cold (water)	**TUC**	Trades Union Congress
HQ	headquarters	**UFO**	unidentified flying object
		UNO	United Nations Organization
		v	versus (against)
		VAT	Value Added Tax
		viz	videlicet (namely)

HE IS A FAMOUS PAINTER.

abstract nouns

An abstract noun is the name of something that can only be thought about and not touched or seen, such as fame, poverty, bravery, happiness, honesty, bluntness. It is called an abstract noun because it names a quality abstracted (that is, taken) from a thing, person or animal. Fame is a quality taken from famous people. It has no existence of its own: it exists only as a way of describing certain people. In the same way you can't have bluntness without blunt things.

The opposite of an abstract noun is a concrete noun*, which names anything (or anyone) that you can actually see and touch.

The commonest endings (suffixes*) of abstract nouns are -ance, -ence, -ery, -ism, -ment, -ness, -sion, -tion, and -ty. These make words such as disturbance, patience, misery, optimism, enjoyment, eagerness, revision, temptation and stupidity.

accent

The word *besides* is made up of two syllables* (be + sides) and the second syllable is spoken more strongly than the first, thus: beSIDES. We say that the accent is on the second syllable.

In the word *tiger* the accent is on the first syllable, thus: TIger. Most words with two syllables have the accent on the first syllable.

In the word *banana* there are three syllables and the accent is on the middle syllable, thus: baNAna.

It is more difficult to know where the stress comes in longer words. Which syllables do you stress in fascination, for instance?

The word 'accent' is also used to describe other ways of pronouncing words differently. So for example we speak of a German accent, a Southern accent, or an Irish accent.

acronyms

When the initials used in an abbreviation* of several words are pronounced as a word, we call the abbreviation an acronym (a first-letters word). Thus Naafi is an acronym for Navy, Army and Air Force Institutes. The word 'radar' was originally an acronym formed from *r*adio *d*etection *a*nd *r*anging.

acrostic

A puzzle or poem in which the first letters of each line make a word or phrase is called an acrostic. In a double acrostic the last letter of each line also forms a word or phrase. Here are two solved acrostics. What other words might fit in place of 'JOCKEY' and 'ROGUE'?

J	O	C	K	E	Y
O	R	D	E	A	L
H	A	S	T	E	N
N	U	M	B	E	R
S	M	O	O	T	H

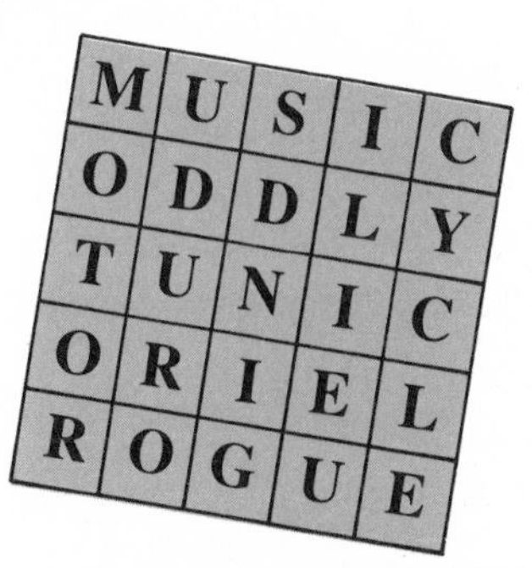

active voice

'To eat' is active, 'to be eaten' is passive. When the subject* of the sentence does something, the verb is usually in the active voice, eg John lit the fire. (The subject, John, does the action.) When something happens to the subject, the verb is usually in the passive voice*. The fire was lit. (The subject, the fire, has the action done to it.)

HE ATE ALL THE CHOCOLATES.

address

Unless they have a special title such as Dr, Col, Sir, Lady or Lord you usually put Mr, Mrs or Miss in front of people's names. The title Ms is often used if you don't know whether a woman is married or unmarried, or if you don't want to make that distinction. Esq after a man's name is still used, especially in business letters, in an attempt to sound polite. Some people address others simply with their first name and surname, eg George Smith. The modern practice is to leave out all inessential punctuation.

13 Appledram Drive
WORLESDON
Suffolk
SL3 9BP

Dear Mr Jones,

Diana Kitson
26 Mill Street
KEIGHLEY
Yorks

Dear Ms Kitson,

adjective

An adjective is a word used to tell us more about what is named by a noun*. It therefore describes creatures, things or ideas. It answers the question, What sort? How many? How much? or Which?

Noun	Adjective
wood	wooden
passion	passionate
snob	snobbish
breath	breathless
care	careful
emotion	emotional
monster	monstrous
muscle	muscular
friend	friendly
water	watery
joy	joyous
lady	ladylike
picture	picturesque
man	manly
metal	metallic

Three adjectives are italicized in this sentence: *Numerous* people buy *these* micros because they are such *reliable* machines.

The adjective *numerous* tells us about the noun 'people' – how many. *These* tells us about the noun 'micros' – which. *Reliable* tells us about the noun 'machines' – what sort.

Many adjectives are formed by adding suffixes* to nouns, eg baby + ish = babyish, hope + less = hopeless.

Other adjectives are formed by adding suffixes to verbs*, eg continue + ous = continuous, eat + able = eatable, possess + ive = possessive, collapse + ible = collapsible.

If an adjective is used too often with the same noun, the combination can become a cliché, eg acid test, giddy heights. Nouns can be used as adjectives, eg television set. See also demonstrative* and possessive* adjectives.

adjective clause

A group of words containing a main verb* and doing the work of an adjective* is called an adjective clause: That is the boy *who scored the winning goal*. The clause* in italics tells us about the noun *boy*. It tells us which boy, and is therefore doing the work of an adjective.

adjective phrase

A group of words without a main verb that does the work of an adjective* is called an adjective phrase: The man *with the shaggy beard* comes from Perth. The italicized group of words is an adjective phrase because it tells us about the noun *man*.

adverb

A word that tells us about the action of a verb* is called an adverb. The most common adverbs tell us when or how an action takes place. They usually end in -ly: Diana skated *superbly* and won the competition. Here the adverb *superbly* tells us about the verb *skated*. It tells us how she skated.

Adverbs may also answer the questions When? Where? How often? How much?, eg

Liz went to a party *yesterday* (When?)

Diana wants to sit *here* (Where?)

John *always* watches this programme (How often?)

They have *half* finished their game (How much?)

Adverbs may also tell us more about adjectives: We are *perfectly* happy. The adverb *perfectly* tells us about the adjective *happy*.

Sometimes adverbs tell us about other adverbs: John played *very* skilfully. The adverb *very* tells us about the adverb *skilfully*: how skilfully?

Adjective	Adverb
swift	swiftly
slow	slowly
easy	easily
angry	angrily
visible	visibly
reliable	reliably
gentle	gently
tame	tamely
brave	bravely
careful	carefully
dull	dully
true	truly
whole	wholly
early	early
right	right

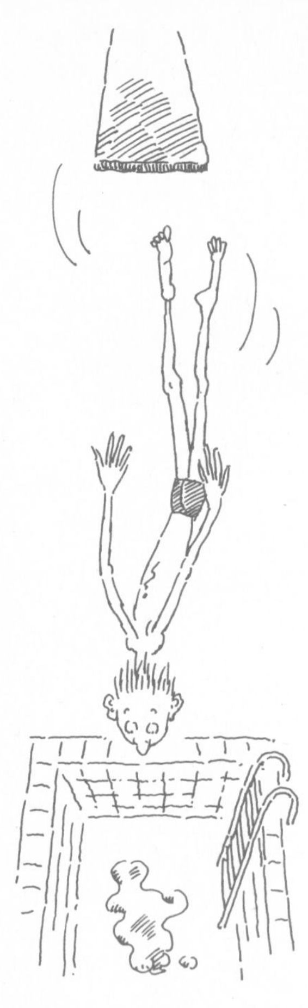

adverb clause

A group of words containing a main verb* and doing the work of an adverb is an adverb clause, eg You should look *before you leap*. The italicized clause tells us about the verb* *should look*. It tells us when you should look.

adverb phrase

A group of words without a main verb* but doing the work of an adverb* is an adverb phrase, eg He acted *in a very careless way*. This adverb phrase tells us about the verb *acted*: it tells us how he acted.

affirmative

This is the opposite of negative*. To answer in the affirmative is to say yes.

agreement

The subject* and verb* must agree. You can't say I goes, or he have. You must say I go, and he has. I am trying; You are trying; He is trying. See also concord*.

alphabetical order

Suppose you want to look a word up in a dictionary, but the words in your dictionary are not listed in any particular order. It might take you all day to find the word you want among the other 10,000 words!

But because the entries are arranged in the same order as the letters of the alphabet, you can find the word you want in a few seconds.

Alphabetical order can be used to arrange other lists too – for example, the names of all the children in your class. How does this work?

If all the words in the list begin with a different letter, you only have to look at their first letters. The word *elbow* will come before *leg* because e comes before l in the alphabet. In the same way *leg* will come before *shoulder*, because l comes before s.

leg	elbow
toe	leg
elbow	shoulder
shoulder	toe

If some of the words begin with the same letter, those words must be arranged according to their second letters. Thus *brooch* will come before *button* because r comes before u.

shirt	brooch
jeans	button
brooch	jeans
button	shirt

When some of the words begin with the same two letters, those words are arranged according to their third letters. Thus *cocoa* comes before *coffee*, because c comes before f.

coffee	cocoa
cream	coffee
cocoa	corn
corn	cream

If in some of the words the first three letters are the same, we must look at the fourth letters. Thus *Smallman* will come before *Smart* because l comes before r. Similarly, *Harding* will come before *Hardman* because i comes before m (fifth letters), and *Hollocks* will come before *Holloway* because c comes before w (sixth letters).

Holloway	Harding
Hardman	Hardman
Smallman	Hollocks
Harding	Holloway
Smart	Smallman
Hollocks	Smart

There is one catch. If one word has the same letters as another but the other goes on further, the shorter one comes before the longer one. Thus *Fowle* will come before *Fowler*, and *Robins* will come before *Robinson*.

Fowle	Fowle
Robinson	Fowler
Fowler	Robins
Robins	Robinson

When several people all have the same surname, we take their first names or the initials of their first names into consideration. Thus *Foley, James* comes before *Foley, John*. In the same way *Foley, R.* comes before *Foley, T.*, and *Foley, T.D.* comes before *Foley, T. J.*

Foley, T.	Foley, James
Foley, T. J.	Foley, John
Foley, T. D.	Foley, R.
Foley, John	Foley, T.
Foley, James	Foley, T. D.
Foley, R.	Foley, T. J.

Can you arrange these lists in alphabetical order?

1.	2.	3.	4.
pear	London	Jacobs	Jones, Simon
apple	Paris	Jackson	Jones, R. H.
plum	Lima	Johnson	Jones, Peter
banana	Madrid	Jagger	Jones, M.
orange	Peking	Jeffrey	Jones, Susan
lemon	Moscow	Johns	Jones, M. J.

ambiguity

This means that something can be taken in two different ways. Ambiguity is usually a sign of bad writing, since the writer has failed to make it clear which meaning is intended. It can also be used humorously, eg A table is wanted by a lady with square legs. Did the writer mean the square legs to belong to the lady or to the table? Presumably to the table, so he should have reworded the advert like this: A table with square legs is wanted by a lady.

The next sentence is ambiguous too, because the words are in the wrong order: She was run over by a car skipping along the road. It could be rewritten without ambiguity thus: Skipping along the road, she was run over by a car.

American	British
apartment	flat
cookies	biscuits
elevator	lift
fall	autumn
faucet	tap
gas(olene)	petrol
truck	lorry

American English

It was in England that the English language first grew up. But it is now spoken by many more people in America than in Britain. American English and British English have kept on growing and changing over the last few centuries, so now they are different in a number of ways.

Americans now say, for instance, Do you have a match? The British usually say, Have you got a match? Americans put their clothes in the 'closet', while the British put them in the wardrobe. Americans walk on the 'sidewalk', while the British walk on the 'pavement'.

anagrams

An anagram is a sort of puzzle. You make a new word by rearranging the letters of another word. Thus, *team* is an anagram of *meat*; *pests* is an anagram of *steps*, and *smear* is an anagram of *mares*. Can you do these anagrams?

1. Change *once* into the fruit of a fir tree.
2. Change *stud* into a kind of fine powder.
3. Change *shrub* into something to paint with.

Word	Anagram
shore	horse
heart	earth
plum	lump
lemon	melon
spear	pears
mane	name
saves	vases

analogies

Just as shoes are to feet, so gloves are to hands. A similarity of this kind, called an analogy, is also often used to explain something less well-known in terms of something more familiar. Any analogy can be stated in this form:

Shoes are to feet as gloves are to hands.
Sheep are to flock as wolves are to pack.
Uncle is to nephew as aunt is to niece.
Paw is to dog as hoof is to horse.

Can you complete these analogies?
1. Swan is to cygnet as duck is to —.
2. Colonel is to — as captain is to navy.
3. Scales are to fish as — are to birds.
4. — is to Britain as Delhi is to India.

anecdote

Any brief account of a remarkable incident is called an anecdote. It may illustrate* some fairly serious idea, or it may just be a funny story. The following anecdote illustrates the idea that there is more to animals than at first appears.

I once stood behind a tree to observe a great crowd of rats marching across a field. While I was watching them I noticed a very strange thing. Two rats passed quite close to my tree, moving more slowly than the rest. There was a small stick between them. Each rat was holding an end of the stick in its mouth. I bent down to see more clearly. Then I understood. The bigger and older rat was blind. The younger rat was leading it with the help of the stick.

Anglo-Saxon

The Angles and Saxons began invading England in the fifth century. In time they settled down as masters of the country. Their language (Anglo-Saxon or Old English) became the language spoken by everyone. It is very different from modern English. It was largely changed by the invasion of the Norman French in 1066, but many Anglo-Saxon words are still used today.

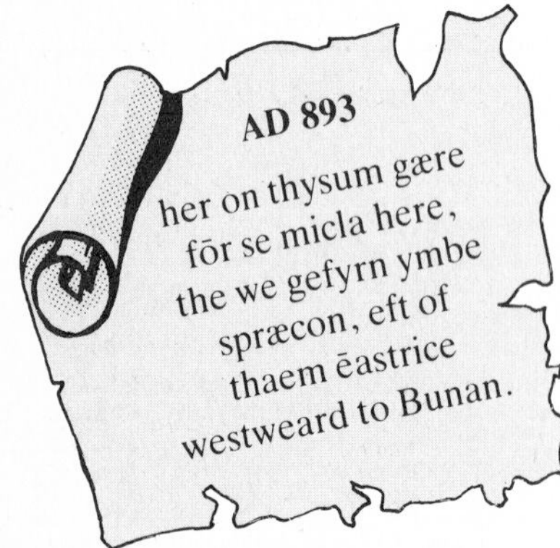

(In this year the great army, that we have already spoken about, came again from the east Kingdom, westward to Boulogne.)

answers

We give answers when we are asked questions. Spoken replies are often one-word answers, eg

'What is his name?' 'Paddy.'

This is more colloquial* than the full answer, 'His name is Paddy.' More often the answer is a short sentence.

'Will you help me?'

'Yes, I will.' (Short for Yes, I will help you.)

But there are some questions to which the answers must be full or long sentences.

'How exactly did he sprain his foot?'

'He fell out of a tree in the park.'

Answers to exam questions are not quite like spoken English and should be a little fuller. You should avoid one-word answers unless you are asked for them. At the same time, examiners will expect natural English, so don't repeat the wording of the question in the answer: Where was the thief when the police arrived? He was in the kitchen. *not* When the police arrived, the thief was in the kitchen.

antonyms

A word which is opposite in meaning to another word is called its antonym. *Sane* is an antonym of *mad*; *forbid* is an antonym of *allow*; *under* is an antonym of *over*. Sometimes the antonym is formed by using a prefix*, eg wise-unwise, appear-disappear.

A true antonym must be the same kind of word, eg newest-oldest (both adjectives*); admits-denies (verbs*); badly-well (adverbs*). *Help* is not an antonym of *unhelpful*, because one is a noun* and the other is an adjective.

Can you think of antonyms for these?

1. clean	4. better	7. never	10. captivity
2. thick	5. success	8. expand	11. enemy
3. shallow	6. succeed	9. obey	12. up

Word	Antonym
slow	quick
clever	stupid
advance	retreat
help	hinder
found	lost
above	below
dwarf	giant
often	seldom
foolishly	wisely

Contraction	Meaning
can't	cannot
doesn't	does not
wouldn't	would not
shan't	shall not
won't	will not
there's	there is
we're	we are
they'll	they will
who'd	who would
it's	it is

apostrophe

This sign, like a comma placed high up, is used in contractions*, eg *don't*. The word *don't* means do not, and the apostrophe shows that a letter (o) has been left out.

The apostrophe is also used to show that someone owns or possesses something:

Steve's nose　　children's clothes
animals' noses　　the chemist's shop

apposition

When two nouns* (or phrases*) are used together to refer to the same person or thing, the second meaning the same but saying it in a different way, we say that they are in apposition, eg Zips, those versatile fasteners, were invented in 1891. The phrase, *those versatile fasteners*, is in apposition to the noun *zips*; they are one and the same thing. Notice that the second item is enclosed by commas*: Paddy, our best batsman, was bowled. The umpire, a girl from Leeds, called him out.

arabic numerals

These are numbers* written in the form 1, 2, 3 etc (as opposed to roman numerals*).

archaism

Any words no longer used in normal English are called archaisms. *Quoth he* (he said), *albeit* (although), and *peradventure* (perhaps) are examples of archaisms. The archaic word *an*, meaning if, survives in the nursery rhyme:

If 'ifs' and 'ans'
Were pots and pans
Where would the tinkers be?

articles

The word *a* (*an*) is called the indefinite article, eg A cow has hoofs. (This is indefinite since 'a' cow might be any cow.)

The definite article (*the*) is so called because when we use it we are definite as to which one we mean, eg The cow over there has a bad hoof. Articles are really very simple adjectives* used to point out 'which'.

Australian English

Just as America and Britain have developed minor differences in their use of English, so too has Australia developed words and expressions that are peculiarly Australian.

Australians speak of the outback; the British call it the countryside. Australians say 'creek', when the British say 'stream', and a 'paddock' to Australians is any field, not just a small enclosure for horses (which is what the word means to the British).

auxiliary verbs

The word *auxiliary* means helping. An auxiliary verb is one that helps the principal verb to form its tense*. A complete English verb is often made up of several words in this way.

Auxiliary verbs		
be	has	might
am	had	can
is	will	could
are	would	do
was	shall	did
were	should	does
have	may	must

have finished	would have finished
will have finished	can be finished
am finishing	will be finished
was finishing	might be finished
did he finish?	may have been finished
has been finished	must have been finished

B

book inscriptions

Books used to be very expensive. Owners did not want them to be stolen and, when they lent a book, they wanted to be sure it would be returned. So the custom grew up of inscribing little doggerel* verses in books, like these:

IF THIS BOOK SHOULD CHANCE TO ROAM,
BOX ITS EARS AND SEND IT HOME.

Small is the wren,
Black is the rook,
Great is the sinner
Who steals this book.

Steal not this book,
My honest friend,
For fear the gallows
Will be your end.

Up the ladder,
Down the rope,
There you'll hang
Until you choke.

brackets

These are punctuation marks – also called parentheses – used to enclose a parenthesis* (words that are not really part of the sentence but an aside to make things clear). The parenthesis in the last sentence, for example, explains the meaning of the word *parenthesis*. In this sentence the parenthesis gives a reason: Please bring an electric drill (ours is out of order), half a bag of cement and a packed lunch.

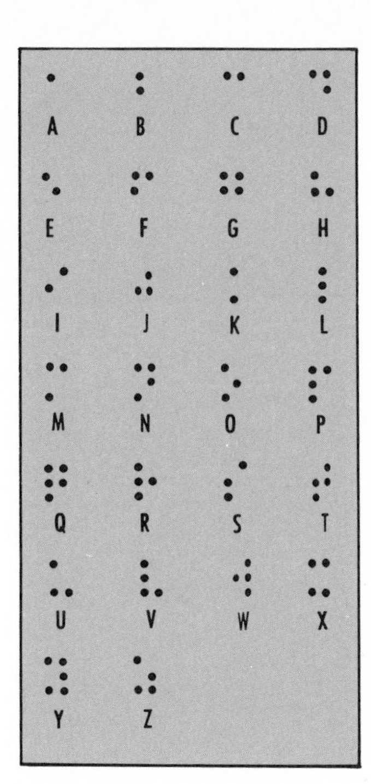

braille

This is a system of printing that enables blind people to read. It uses raised dots that you can feel with your fingers, instead of letters.

buildings

There are many special names for buildings which tell you what they are used for:

bakery	a place where bread is made
castle	formerly the fortified home of a noble
cathedral	the chief church of a diocese
convent	a place where nuns live
granary	a storehouse for grain
mint	a place where money is coined
silo	a tower where crops are stored for fodder
tannery	a factory where leather is made

Do you know what these are called?

1. A building where goods are stored
2. A house to keep pigs
3. A place where beer is made
4. A large building for quartering troops
5. A place where monks live

building words

There are three main ways of building words. You can add prefixes*, suffixes*, or another word (making compound words*).

Prefixes: vision, revision, television
Suffixes: care, careless, careful, caring
Compounds: blackbird, mudguard, hard-working

All the derivatives* you can build from one root word make up a word family*. The changes are called inflexions*.

business letters

Because in business you are unlikely to be on intimate terms with your correspondent, business letters are more formal than personal letters*. It is still usual to begin with Dear Sir, or Dear Madam, and end with Yours faithfully or Yours truly. But nowadays, once a firm has your name, its letter writer is quite likely to address you as Mr So-and-so or Ms So-and-so, and may end the letter Yours sincerely. Unlike personal letters, the name and address of the firm you are writing to is written on the left before the salutation*.

13 Appledram Drive
WORLESDON
Suffolk
SL1 7HE

25th September 1985

he Manager
Lloyds Bank PLC
64 Thurston Road
EAST METTERHAM
Suffolk
SL3 9BP

Dear Sir,

Current Account No. 90889653

Please credit the enclosed cheque to my acc
send me an up-to-date statement.

I should also like to have information abo
a deposit account.

Yours faithfully,

(S N Jones)

26 Mill Street
KEIGHLEY
Yorks

25th September

The Secretary
Computer Supplies Ltd
81 Forest Road
HARLOW
Essex

Dear Sir,

The Micro Computer I bought from you last December has broken down. The numbers on the calculator pad print up wrong on the screen.

Should I send it to you for repair, or take it to a local dealer and send you the bill? The machine is still under guarantee.

Yours faithfully,

Diana Kitson

capital letters

Capital letters are used:

1. To begin every sentence:
   This is the first example.
2. For the word I:
   Oh, I could have bitten off my tongue!
3. To begin all first names and surnames:
   George Thompson, Elizabeth Macdonald
4. For a person's initials:
   R. J. Smith, G. K. Chesterton, R.L.S.
5. To begin all proper nouns*:

Canada	Thames	High Street
Melbourne	Himalayas	Piccadilly
H.M.S. Victory	Eton College	Rex Cinema

6. To begin all adjectives* formed from proper nouns:

British (Britain)	Victorian (Victoria)
Jamaican (Jamaica)	Cornish (Cornwall)
Christian (Christ)	Buddhist (Buddha)

7. To begin the names of the days, months and special holidays:
   Tuesday, September, Easter, Boxing Day
8. To begin the main words in the titles of books, plays, newspapers, poems and songs:
   The Wind in the Willows
   The Pirates of Penzance
   News of the World
   Green Grow the Rushes – Oh!
9. To begin the first word of direct speech*:
   She said 'Good luck, my son.'
   'Good luck, my son,' she said.
10. For official titles:
    Her Royal Highness The Duke of Edinburgh
    Lord Glenconner The Archbishop of York
11. To begin the word God and words meaning the one God, and pronouns* standing for God, especially in Christian literature:
    He, the Almighty, the Lord, Allah
12. Usually to begin each line of poetry.

I reckon a nose
Is as long as it grows,
But why does an elephant's
Reach down to its toes?
Who knows?

Spelling	
2	two
8	eight
12	twelve
18	eighteen
31	thirty-one
75	seventy-five
497	four hundred and ninety-seven

cardinal numbers

The simple numbers such as one, two, three, twenty-two, forty-nine, a thousand, are called cardinal (chief) numbers to distinguish them from ordinal (order-showing) numbers such as first, second, third, twenty-first, forty-ninth, thousandth. Notice that numbers such as twenty-six or fifty-eight are written with a hyphen.

case

The form of a noun* or pronoun* that shows its relation to other words in the sentence is called its case, eg *He* chased *him* because he had taken *Jim's* balloon. Here the pronoun *He* is the subject* of the verb *chased* and is said to be in the nominative* case. The pronoun *him* is the object* of the verb *chased* and is said to be in the objective* (or accusative) case. The noun *Jim's* shows possession and is said to be in the genitive or possessive case*.

catchwords

A catchword is a word or phrase that takes people's fancy for a while and is repeated frequently and without much thought till it goes out of fashion. Some recently fashionable catchwords include 'Nice one Cyril!', and 'So-and-so rules OK'.

centuries

We have to think very clearly when dealing with a particular century (a period of 100 years). For example, we are now living in the twentieth century, and the year 1851 was in the nineteenth century, *not* in the eighteenth century.

You can see why this is so if you go back to the beginning of the centuries AD (after Christ).

The years 1–99 were obviously the first century. The years 100–199 were therefore the second century, and so on.

classification

Any noun* that names something that includes a number of kinds is said to name a class or be a class name. Thus *vehicles* is the class name that includes cars, buses, lorries, coaches, trains. In the same way plates, cups, bowls and jugs belong to the class called *crockery*, while violins, cellos, guitars and banjos all belong to the class called *stringed instruments.*

When you put things into classes like this, you classify them. The act of classifying is called classification. You can also classify words according to whether they are nouns*, verbs*, adjectives*, adverbs*, conjunctions*, prepositions* or exclamations*.

Can you classify these groups?

1. water, oil, wine, milk, vinegar
2. dagger, gun, spear, sword, lance
3. kittens, cygnets, foals, joeys, cubs, kids
4. socks, shirts, pullovers, jackets, hats, overalls
5. India, Canada, Australia, Jamaica, New Zealand
6. lizards, snakes, crocodiles, tortoises

clauses

A clause is a group of words, including a main verb*, which can do the work of a noun*, an adverb* or an adjective in the sentence. As it has a subject* and a predicate*, a clause taken out of a sentence may become a complete sentence by itself. A clause like this is called a main clause. This sentence contains three clauses: I went straight to the beach / because I was late / and my friends would be waiting for me. The first clause is the main clause, because it could also stand on its own as a complete sentence: I went straight to the beach.

clichés

Any overworked word* or expression is called a cliché, eg 'as good as gold', 'way out', 'like anything', or 'I mean to say!' Clichés pass muster in conversation, but in writing we have time to think of something less stale.

codes

In a general sense a code is any system of symbols. The English alphabet is a code; it is a set of symbols that everyone agrees to use in a certain way to make reading possible. Some alphabets are entirely different from the roman alphabet used in English, but to the people in the countries using them, the symbols represent certain sounds and so make reading in their language just as easy.

There are other agreed codes. Morse code* is a method of communication in which letters and numbers are represented by dots and dashes.

You can signal with Morse code by flashing a light, by sound or by waving a flag. The dots are as short as possible, and the dashes three times as long in order to distinguish them. Here is a message in Morse code:

–·–· ––– –– · ·– – ––– –· –·–· ·

This is deciphered as: Come at once.

The semaphore code is a means of signalling by holding flags in various positions to indicate letters and numbers. Braille* is a code using raised dots to enable blind people to read.

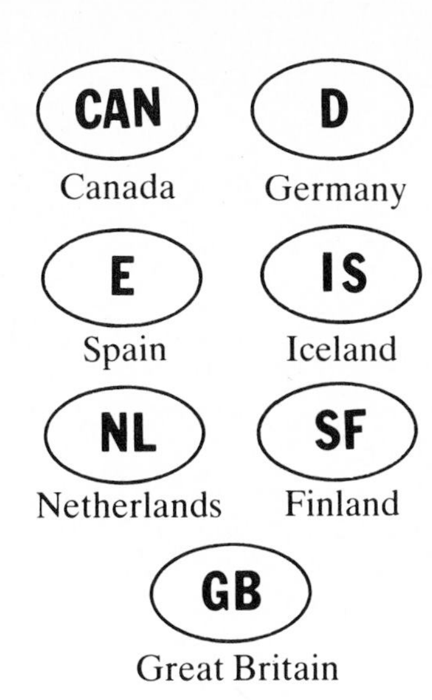

Then there are International Vehicle Registration Letters. These use capital letters to indicate the country of origin of the vehicle.

The word 'code' is also used to mean a system of secret writing. Here is a message written in a very simple secret code:

You can decipher the message by means of the code, which was formed by making each letter of the alphabet stand for the letter before it in the alphabet:

a	b	c	d	e	f	g	h	i	j	k	l	m	n	o	p	q	r	s	t	u	v	w	x	y	z
z	a	b	c	d	e	f	g	h	i	j	k	l	m	n	o	p	q	r	s	t	u	v	w	x	y

collective nouns

When a noun* names a collection of creatures or things, we call it a collective noun. We speak of a *band* of musicians, a *herd* of cows, a *suite* of furniture, a *pack* of cards, a *clump* of trees. The words *band*, *herd*, *suite*, *pack*, *clump* are all collective nouns.

It is important to remember that a collective noun names a single collection. There may be many in the collection, but there is only one collection. The collective noun is therefore singular. So we say: There is a band in the park every other Saturday (*is*: singular). Sometimes,

a board of directors
a company of actors
a flock of sheep
a gaggle of geese
a gang of thieves
a litter of puppies
a cluster of stars
a flight of aeroplanes
a set of golf-clubs
a pack of wolves
a plague of locusts
a swarm of bees
a pride of lions

however, we do not think of the collection as a single whole. Instead we think of the many individual people or things that make up the whole. When we do this, we can treat the collective noun as if it were plural: All the band are young men from the village (*are*: plural).

What are collections of these called?		
1. singers	4. cattle	7. ships
2. sailors	5. cubs	8. tools
3. birds	6. grapes	9. fish

colloquial language

Language used in free and easy conversation, but not on polite or formal occasions, is called colloquial. It generally uses more colourful, idiomatic expressions. Here are some examples of colloquialisms and their polite alternatives:

hard up – short of money
stuck up – snobbish
a wet blanket – a discouraging person
dead beat – exhausted
a chip off the old block – very like father
at a loose end – with nothing to do
out of sorts – not feeling well
to sling mud – to slander
to chew the fat – to argue
to send him packing – to dismiss him quickly
to be down in the mouth – to be in low spirits
to take a rise out of – to fool

colons

The main use of this punctuation mark (:) is to indicate that 'as follows' is meant, eg The countries visited were: Austria, Belgium, Denmark, Norway, Finland, Spain and Portugal. Sometimes, especially if the words 'as follows' are written, a dash is added to the colon(:-), eg The order of the draw was as follows:- John, Lucy, Anne, Michael, Steve, Margaret.

commands

A sentence that tells you to do something is called a command. It uses the imperative* form of the verb.

Go away.

Be off with you!

See if the lights have been switched off, John.

A polite order is usually called a request.

Would you mind fetching my book, please, John.

I wonder if you would hold this for me, John.

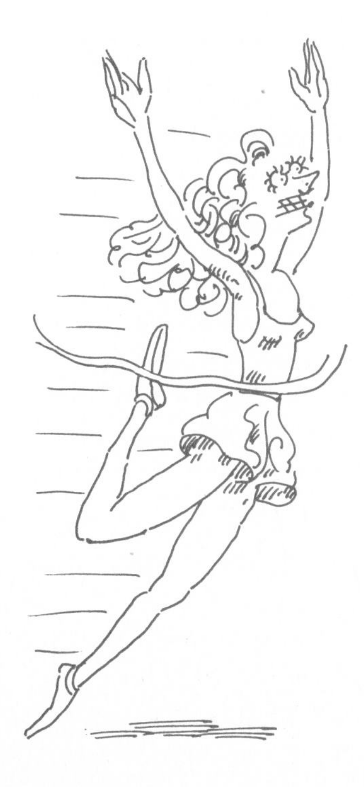

commas

These punctuation marks (,) are used:

1. To separate words arranged as a series. These are usually nouns* or adjectives*:
   There were carrots, turnips, lettuces, cabbages and tomatoes beautifully arranged for sale.
   The dancing was lively, enthusiastic, skilful and graceful.
2. To separate phrases* or clauses*:
   We looked for it in the car, in the shed, under the bed, behind the cupboard and in the garden, but couldn't find it anywhere.
   John ran down the lane, opened the gate, crossed the field and climbed up the old oak tree.
3. To separate words in apposition*:
   I was glad that Diana, my sister, won the race.

4. To separate the person addressed from the rest of the sentence:
   'John, remember to ring Mr Ash!' said Mrs Jones.
5. To mark off phrases* beginning with a participle*:
   The first runner, puffed already, was beginning to slow up. Following close behind him, Mike looked the likely winner.
6. To end direct speech* when no question mark or exclamation mark is needed:
   'This looks like the winner,' said Barbara.
7. To mark off sentence adverbs* from the rest of the sentence:
   Nevertheless, the result was very close. We all thought, as a matter of fact, that Mike would win.

common nouns

A common noun names any one of a class of persons or things, while a proper noun* names a specific person or thing. Thus, *woman* is a common noun because it names a class of persons called woman. But *Mrs Smith* is a proper noun because it names one specific individual.

Common	Proper
boy	Steve
man	Mr Jones
country	France
city	London
mountain	Snowdon
river	Niger

comparative adjectives

tall	taller
thin	thinner
polite	politer
angry	angrier
casual	more casual
slipshod	more slipshod
beautiful	more beautiful
far	further
bad	worse

The comparative is that form of an adjective or adverb used to express 'more'. Short adjectives form their comparative by adding -er, eg slow-slower, early-earlier. But some adjectives of two syllables* that cannot be easily pronounced when -er is added, and all words of three or more syllables, form their comparative by using *more*, eg loyal – more loyal, intelligent – more intelligent. A few are irregular, eg good – better, little – less. Sometimes the spelling is changed a bit when -er is added, eg late – later (not lateer), early – earlier (not earlyer).

comparative adverbs

A few short adverbs, such as fast, hard, early, quick, form their comparative by adding -er in the same way as comparative adjectives*, eg John worked harder and faster than all the others. Most adverbs, however, form their comparative by using 'more': rapidly – more rapidly, formally – more formally. A few adverbs have an irregular comparative: well – better, badly – worse, far – further.

complement

Verbs like to be, to become, to seem, or to look, usually need a word to complete them.

He is . . . (incomplete)
She seems . . . (incomplete)
The flowers look . . . (incomplete)
He is an expert (complete)
She seems honest (complete)
The flowers look pretty (complete)

The words that complete these incomplete* verbs are called the complement. *An expert*, *honest* and *pretty* are complements in the sentences above.

compositions

Any continuous piece of writing of more than a line or two may be called a composition. Stories, descriptions*, explanations, accounts, letters*, instructions, diaries, anecdotes* and essays* are all different kinds of composition.

The basic skills required for a good composition include correct spelling, effective punctuation, varied sentence construction and acceptable language use (grammar); also variety of expression (literal and figurative*), appropriate language, sound paragraphing*, and a clear overall structure. Beyond these basic skills, the quality of the composition will depend upon the writer's knowledge and imagination.

compound words

When two or more distinct words are joined together to make a single word, we call it a compound word.

bed + room = bedroom
rain + bow = rainbow
left + handed = left-handed
under + done = underdone
good + looking = good-looking
walking + stick = walking-stick
father + in + law = father-in-law

Most compound words are either nouns* or adjectives*. Notice that some are hyphenated. There is no firm rule about using the hyphen. On the whole, the more accepted and common the word, the more likely it is to be written without a hyphen. On the other hand, most adjectives retain the hyphen: quick-witted, house-proud, fair-headed, long-playing, tongue-tied, hard-working.

Some compound nouns

toothache
lighthouse
quicksilver
flyover
layby
roundabout
pickup
outlaw
onlooker
letter-box
swimming-pool
son-in-law
man-of-war
walk-over

computer English

There are special 'languages', such as BASIC and COBOL, which people can use to operate a computer. These might be considered special kinds of code*, which the human user can understand and to which the machine can respond.

concord

This is a more formal word for agreement*. Subject* and verb*, demonstrative adjective* and noun*, possessive noun* and the number of people possessing must be in concord, eg 'He eat', 'this apples', 'their nose' are not in agreement; 'he eats', 'these apples', 'their noses' are in agreement.

concrete noun

The word *concrete* means really existing in a material sense – having weight and occupying space. So a concrete noun names something that can be seen, touched or weighed. It is the opposite of an abstract noun*, which names something that only exists as a thought. Thus *coward* is a concrete noun, while *cowardice* is an abstract noun. In the same way *feather* is a concrete noun, but *featheriness* is an abstract noun.

LATE NIGHT HORROR

STEVE IS A COWARD.

condition See *'if' sentences**

confused words

Words in English can be confused if they sound alike (homophones*), eg beech-beach, bear-bare, board-bored, creak-creek, right-write. They can also be confused if they are spelt alike (homonyms*), eg *bow* (a knot) and *bow* (to bend), *lead* (a leash) and *lead* (a metal).

Some conjunctions	
and	since
but	because
or	until
if	although
when	unless
before	while
either . . . or	after

conjunctions

Words that join parts of the sentence are called conjunctions. They may join single words, eg salt *and* pepper. They may join phrases*, eg by car *or* on foot. They may also join two clauses*: We lost *because* we had not trained well enough. Notice that a conjunction still joins the two clauses even when it comes at the beginning of the sentence: *Because* we had not trained well enough, we lost.

consonants

A sound made by checking or stopping the breath as it passes through the mouth is called a consonant. Consonant sounds are represented by all the letters of the alphabet except a,e,i,o,u, which represent vowel* sounds.

Container	Contents
briefcase	documents
bunker	coal
caddy	tea
carafe	wine
compact	face-powder
holster	pistol

containers

English is rich in special names for containers. Large quantities of beer are kept in barrels but rainwater is kept in a butt. Picnics are often put in a hamper, while a punnet would probably contain fresh strawberries. What would the following probably contain?

1. hangar	3. cruet	5. envelope	7. carton
2. wardrobe	4. safe	6. scabbard	8. urn

context

Words can often have more than one meaning. The context, that is, the surrounding words and the situation in which they are spoken or written, will usually make clear which meaning is intended, eg The population around Birmingham is very dense. There are more people per square mile there than in almost any other part of Britain.

If you quoted the first sentence, leaving out the second and so taking it out of its context, it would look as if you were insulting the people by calling them dense.

contractions

Words that have been shortened by the omission of one or more letters are called contractions. The missing letters are usually indicated by apostrophes*. Contractions are regularly used in conversation, even on formal occasions. They are normal in informal writing too. Indeed, the commonest, such as can't, don't, doesn't, didn't, wouldn't, couldn't, are becoming acceptable in fairly formal writing in newspapers, magazines and novels. When a more formal tone to your writing is required, however, they should be avoided, though in dialogue* they can be used to represent normal speech.

Some Contractions	
couldn't	could not
didn't	did not
hasn't	has not
he'd	he would
he'll	he will
I'll	I will
I'd	I had
isn't	is not
it's	it is
I've	I have
that's	that is
who's	who has
you're	you are

conversation

When conversation is written down, it is called dialogue*, and it is punctuated with inverted commas*.

correct English

The rules of English are not often definite enough for us to talk about correct and incorrect English. It is largely a question of suitability. If the language is intelligible and suited to the occasion (polite when politeness is required, standard English* at school, informal among friends), then it is probably all right. When you're just having a chat, the rules aren't so important. But when you want to be precise, and especially in writing, there are some common pitfalls to watch out for.

WHERE ARE THE OTHER LEG OF MY JEANS?

It could, for instance, make a bad impression if you say 'He done it' when you mean 'He did it', or 'He has broke his leg' when you mean 'He has broken his leg', or 'He couldn't remember nothing' when you mean 'He couldn't remember anything', or 'Where is my jeans?' when you mean 'Where are my jeans?'.

This sort of mistake is dealt with under agreement*, ambiguity*, confused words*, homonyms*, homophones*. In writing, of course, mistakes can also be made in spelling*, punctuation* and the use of capitals*.

correspondence

This is the term used to include all kinds of message sent by post or by hand, such as business letters*, personal letters*, invitations* or announcements.

cross reference

A reference from one part of a book to another is called a cross reference. If you look up *concord* in this book, for example, you will find a cross reference to *agreement*. The asterisk (*) after *agreement* means that you should refer to *agreement* for further information. In many books the cross reference is made by adding *q.v.* after the word, meaning 'which see' (*quod vide*).

crossword puzzles

Across
10 A baby cat

Down
7 The opposite of *starts*

A completed crossword puzzle can be read across and down. That is to say, all the letters across must make words, as must the letters down. You find out the words required by following the clues, and then you write one letter of the word in each square, starting at the number indicated and going across or down according to the instructions. If you are not already a crossword puzzle solver, you will learn quickly by studying the clues of these puzzles, which have been solved for you.

CLUES

Across

2. A person who goes for a long walk
4. The opposite of *nasty*
6. You play tennis with it.
7. You smooth clothes with it.
8. A row of seats in a series of banked rows
9. A synonym* for *bigger*
11. They are filled with meat or fruit.
12. An antonym* for *starts*

Down

1. The first letters of your names
2. A large wading bird with long neck and legs
3. The largest kind of deer
5. A sea animal shaped like a five-pointed star
8. Short for *turpentine*
10. Decay

CLUES

Across

1. Large ponds
5. A cover for the top of a container
6. An antonym* for *near*
8. An animal story teaching a lesson

Down

2. It unlocks doors
3. A synonym* for *stomach*
4. A container for money
7. A baby lion

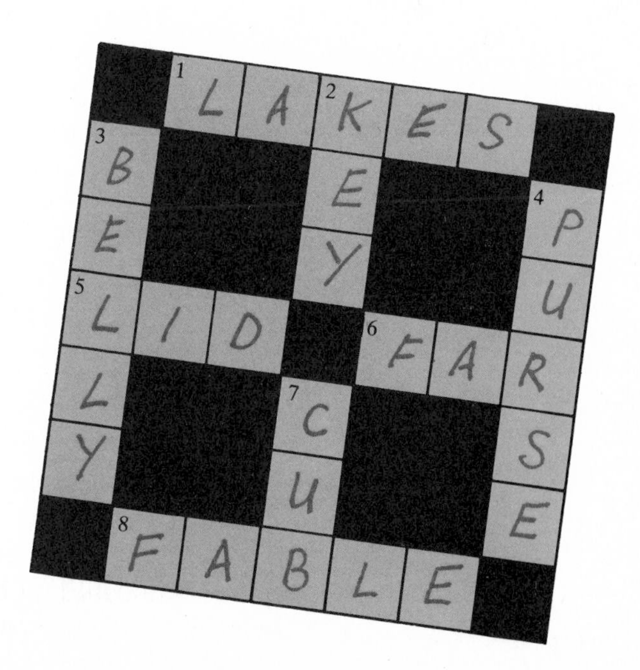

countries

It is important to be able to spell the names of countries and to know the adjective* that is formed from each name. The language spoken in a country is sometimes (but not always) named from the adjective. We speak of Chinese crackers (adjective), and Chinese (the language), and of Mexican sombreros (adjective), but the language of Mexico is Spanish. Notice that all adjectives formed from the names of countries begin with a capital letter*, and so do the names of languages.

Country	Adjective	Main Languages
Australia	Australian	English
Barbados	Barbadian	English
Belgium	Belgian	Flemish & French
Canada	Canadian	English & French
Denmark	Danish	Danish
Egypt	Egyptian	Arabic
France	French	French
Ghana	Ghanaian	English
Greece	Greek	Greek
Iceland	Icelandic	Icelandic
India	Indian	Hindi & English
Ireland	Irish	English & Erse
Israel	Israeli	Hebrew
Italy	Italian	Italian
Jamaica	Jamaican	English
Malta	Maltese	Maltese & English
Netherlands	Dutch	Dutch
Nigeria	Nigerian	English
Pakistan	Pakistani	Urdu & English
Portugal	Portuguese	Portuguese
Russia	Russian	Russian
Switzerland	Swiss	German & French
Trinidad	Trinidadian	English
United States	American	English

dashes

The dash is a form of punctuation that may be used:

1. Instead of brackets* to enclose a parenthesis*:
   My grandfather – he was a very brave man – sailed across the Atlantic single-handed.
2. Instead of commas* to mark off words in apposition*:
   With our present choir – twenty first-class singers – we are much in demand.
3. To indicate a blank (a word or letters omitted):
   It was not until 1982 that I met Mr C—.
4. To separate repeated words:
   The deal was accompanied by a promise – a promise that was never kept.

dates

Months of the Year	
Jan	January
Feb	February
Mar	March
Apr	April
May	May
Jun	June
Jul	July
Aug	August
Sep	September
Oct	October
Nov	November
Dec	December

The most convenient way of setting out the date is like this: 21st June 1985.

Long month names may be abbreviated: 10th Dec. 1986. A fairly common way of writing the date is thus: Dec. 10th, 1986.

It is less convenient because it needs a comma* to prevent the numbers getting confused. This is especially so if, as is becoming the custom, the ordinal* number is written without st, th, nd: Dec. 10, 1986. It is easier to read like this: 10 Dec. 1986.

When you read the date aloud, it must be read in full, eg 'the tenth of December nineteen hundred and eighty-six'. The 'hundred and' may be omitted as it is obviously understood.

Dates can also be written in figures only, eg 10.12.86. This too can be confusing, as Americans put the number of the month first: 12.10.86. To the British this would mean 12th October 1986.

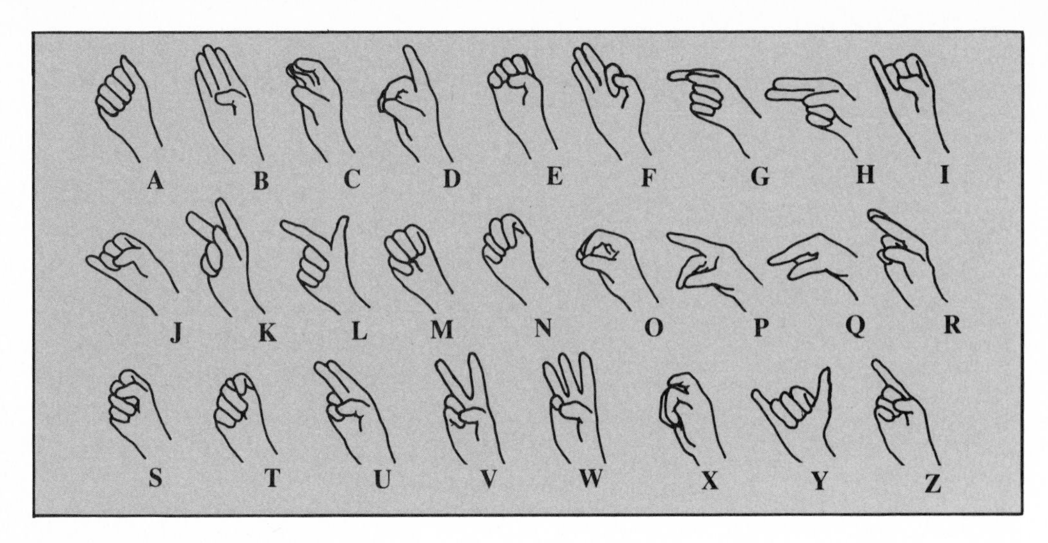

deaf and dumb alphabet

This consists of different positions of the fingers and hands to represent letters and words so that a deaf and dumb person can communicate with other people. It is of course a kind of code*.

definite article

There are two articles*. The definite article is *the*, and the indefinite article is *a*.

definitions

The definition of a word is an exact statement of its meaning. This is a definition of a boomerang: A boomerang is a curved throwing stick, used as a weapon by the Australian Aborigines, that flies back to the thrower if it fails to hit its target.

In defining a word, you must take great care to limit its meaning so that it means what you are defining and nothing else. It is no good defining *cat* as a small animal; there are thousands of small animals. Nor do we limit the meaning to a cat if we call it a small fur-covered mammal, since there are still a lot of small fur-covered mammals. But we shall be limiting the meaning

fairly exactly if we say: A cat is a small fur-covered mammal that purrs and is often kept as a pet.

Notice that when we are defining a noun* (boomerang, cat), we must say what class of thing it belongs to (throwing stick, mammal) and also what makes it possible to distinguish it from others in its class – curved, used by Aborigines, returns to its thrower in the case of the boomerang; small, fur-covered, purrs, kept as a pet in the case of the cat. It is similar when you define a verb*: To whisper means to speak very softly so as not to be overheard.

First you have the general class of action (speak), then what distinguishes it from other forms of speaking (softly, in order not to be overheard).

In defining adjectives, we have to explain the meaning in as simple a way as possible:

edible, able and fit to be eaten

populous, thickly populated; having a lot of people living there

unabridged, not shortened; in full

well-meaning, having good intentions

The definitions of adverbs* must be simple explanations of the meaning in the same way:

bumptiously, in a very self-important way

contemptuously, in a way showing contempt or scorn

hastily, in a quick or hurried way

A dictionary* is full of definitions aimed at making the meanings of words clear. Of what words are these the definitions? (The answers all begin with *c*.)

1. badly or abnormally shaped
2. to break into crumbs
3. a word used to join parts of a sentence
4. a likeness so exaggerated as to be ridiculous

demonstrative adjectives

An adjective* that points out the thing or creature named by a noun* is called a demonstrative adjective.

this dog *these* dogs
that cat *those* cats

demonstrative pronouns

A pronoun* that points out the thing or creature named by the noun it stands for is called a demonstrative pronoun.

This is my watch. *That* is the anchor. *These* are the life-jackets. *Those* are the sails.

A demonstrative pronoun stands on its own in place of a noun. It should not be confused with the demonstrative adjective*, which is always accompanied by the noun it describes.

derivations

The derivation of a word tells you where it came from. The word fight derives from the Anglo-Saxon *feoht*. Over a period of hundreds of years both the pronunciation and the spelling have changed. Other words derived from Anglo-Saxon, with their original Anglo-Saxon in brackets, include: and (*ond*), flee (*flie*), slay (*slaegen*), thousand (*thusend*).

Many other words came into the language with the arrival of the Norman French, who settled in England after defeating King Harold in 1066. For example, the English originally just called mutton 'sheep', but when the meat was served up on the table of their Norman French masters it was called by its French name *mouton*. This name eventually became the modern word mutton. The derivations of pork, beef and veal are similar. They come from the French names for the animals known in Anglo-Saxon

English as swine (*porc*), cow (*boeuf*), and calf (*veau*).

Many modern English words derive directly from Latin. Most of them were borrowed during the Middle Ages when all serious education was carried on in Latin. Right up to about 1550, Latin was the language of instruction in the few Grammar Schools in England. Many Latin words found their way into the language as a result. They were mostly the more sophisticated words for which there was no equivalent in the cruder English of those days, such as: accommodate, capacious, compute, distinguish, estimate, experiment, investigate, manuscript, radius.

Modern English derives from many other languages, as can be seen from these examples:

drudge (Celtic)	deck (Dutch)	shawl (Persian)
drama (Greek)	bungalow (Hindi)	armada (Spanish)
paragraph (Greek)	tundra (Russian)	bantam (Malay)
replica (Italian)	plunder (German)	blarney (Irish)
etiquette (French)	almanac (Arabic)	coffee (Turkish)

derivatives

When a word is borrowed from another language, we say that it derives from that language. Its original form in that language is called its derivation*. You can build new words from English words too: new words made in this way are called derivatives. Derivatives are formed mainly by means of prefixes* and suffixes*. Derivatives of 'sure' include: unsure (prefix added), surely, sureness, surest (suffixes added), unsureness (prefix and suffix added).

The root word and its derivatives are sometimes called a word family*.

descriptions

The secret of a good description is to choose only those points that help to give a clear picture of what you are describing. If you want to describe a tidy room, for example, you will do best to choose those features of the room that will emphasize that it is a tidy room. The number of windows will be irrelevant. In the same way, if you want to describe an ugly person, you should concentrate on the various ways in which the person is ugly.

A description can be done briefly in a single paragraph*, as with Dickens's description of a schoolroom (from *Nicholas Nickleby*) on the next page, or it can be done more fully. A description of a person might be divided into three parts: appearance, character, behaviour. In that case you would devote one paragraph to each aspect and, in order to weld all three into one whole, you would take care to see that there is a natural link* between paragraphs.

The description of a bread-fruit tree, adapted from Ballantyne's *Coral Island*, is a complete composition in four paragraphs. The first one introduces the tree and describes its leaves. The second, with a simple link* ('The tree') to connect with the first, deals with its fruit. The third paragraph, linked simply with 'The trunk', describes the importance of the wood. The concluding paragraph is firmly linked to the whole subject matter by 'With such beauty and usefulness'.

Dotheboy's Hall

It was a bare and dirty room, with a couple of windows, of which a tenth part might be glass, the remainder being stopped up with copybooks and paper. There were a couple of long old rickety desks, cut and notched, and inked and damaged in every possible way, two or three forms, a detached desk for Mr Squeers, and another for his assistant. The ceiling was supported, like that of a barn, by cross beams and rafters; and the walls were so stained and discoloured that it was impossible to tell whether they had ever been touched with paint or whitewash.

The Bread-fruit Tree

On our walk across the tropical island, we came upon a bread-fruit tree and stopped to examine it carefully. We were much struck with its broad leaves, which were twelve or eighteen inches long, deeply indented, and of a glossy smoothness, like the laurel.

The tree bears two or three crops of fruit in a year. It is round in shape, about six inches in diameter, and it has a rough rind. It forms the principal food of many South Sea Islanders. The fruit on the tree which we inspected hung in clusters of twos and threes, and were of various colours, from light pea-green to brown and rich yellow. The yellow fruit was the ripe fruit.

The trunk was twenty feet high, being quite destitute of branches up to that height, where it branched off into a beautiful head. The wood, which is durable and of a good colour, is used to build native houses. The bark of the young branches is made into cloth.

With such beauty and usefulness, it is no wonder that the bread-fruit tree is highly regarded. We were lucky indeed to find such trees growing on our island.

dialect

The type of speech that is peculiar to a certain district is called a dialect. People in that district use some words and idioms* that are not part of standard English*, and they probably pronounce most of their words with a different accent* too.

In Britain, Cockney is a dialect of a certain part of London, while Lancashire has an easily recognized dialect too. Scottish dialect is a major dialect, whereas Glaswegian English is a subdivision of the Scottish dialect.

In a less obvious way, most counties in Britain have their own dialects, the most noticeable differences from standard English being in vowel sounds and intonation*.

Thus, a person from Somerset would speak in a way that a person from Yorkshire would at once recognize as being different from his way of speaking.

But dialect is almost entirely a matter of speech. In writing, there is rarely much difference between the English of one county and another; everyone writes in the standard English they were taught at school. Just occasionally a dialect is used in writing, for example in Burns's *Auld Lang Syne*:

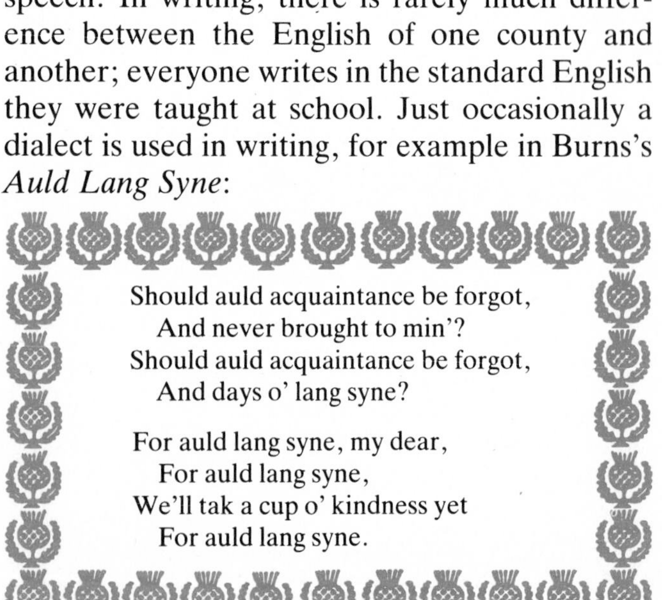

Should auld acquaintance be forgot,
   And never brought to min'?
Should auld acquaintance be forgot,
   And days o' lang syne?

For auld lang syne, my dear,
   For auld lang syne,
We'll tak a cup o' kindness yet
   For auld lang syne.

dialogue

Written conversation is usually referred to as dialogue and set down with quotation marks*.

'Tell me what happened,' he said. 'I want the truth.'

Dialogue also refers to spoken conversation, especially in plays, where it is set down like this:

Mrs Jones What can I do to help, Officer?

Policeman I need to know the names of your guests.

dictionaries

A dictionary may be defined as a reference book* giving words in alphabetical order with their meanings. It may also give their pronunciation, part of speech*, etymology*, and derivatives*.

diminutives

A booklet is a little book, and a duckling is a little or baby duck. Words like *booklet* and *duckling* are called diminutives.

Diminutives are usually formed by adding suffixes*, but the prefix* *mini-* has also become popular in recent years.

-let eaglet, leaflet, owlet, rivulet, piglet
-ling duckling, gosling, seedling
-et coronet, locket, leveret, cygnet
-ette cigarette, rosette, kitchenette, epaulette
-kin manikin, lambkin
-ock bullock, hillock
mini- miniskirt, minibus, minicar

There are also special words for small quantities . Thus we talk of a *puff* of wind, a *wisp* of smoke, a *grain* of sand, and a *crumb* of bread.

Diminutive	Meaning
leveret	baby hare
cygnet	baby swan
coronet	little crown
rivulet	little river
nestling	baby bird
elver	baby eel

diphthongs

When two vowel sounds glide together to form one sound, we have what is called a diphthong. Thus, the *oi* sound in *point* is made up of the *aw* sound in *jaw* and the *i* sound in *fit*. Other diphthongs are:

ow as in *flower*
u as in *cube*
i as in *fine*

directions

Directions sometimes have to be written down, especially when you are telling someone in a letter how to find your house. More often they have to be given orally when strangers ask you to tell them the way. Directions should be kept as brief as possible so as not to confuse your inquirer. Another useful hint is to mention the buildings or landmarks they will pass on the way, as they will help them check that they are going the right way.

> Mr Fulton was in West Street when the man asked him the way to the swimming pool. These are the directions he gave:
>
> 'Go along this road till you come to the crossroads, where you will see a set of traffic lights. Turn right at the lights. Go along that road, passing the Post Office on your left, till the road forks. Take the left-hand fork and go for about 200 metres. You will pass a church on your right and shortly afterwards you will see a turning to the left called New Road. The swimming pool is about 50 metres along New Road on the left. You can't miss it: there's a big notice up outside the entrance.'

Points of the Compass	
N	north
NE	north-east
NW	north-west
NNE	north-north-east
E	east
S	south
SW	south-west
SE	south-east
SSW	south-south-west
W	west

Can you describe the route from your home to the nearest bookshop?

direct speech

Words written down exactly as they are spoken are called direct speech. The words actually spoken are enclosed in quotation marks*, which are also known as inverted commas*. Any words not actually spoken (he said, she asked politely, etc) are kept outside the quotation marks:

'Where is Glasgow, John?' asked Mrs Jones.

'It's in the south of Scotland,' he replied.

Notice that the spoken words are separated from the unspoken words by a question mark if it is a question, and by a comma if it is not. When there are no unspoken words, the full stop comes inside the quotation marks:

'Now let's hear your story,' Mr Fulton said. 'I want all the facts.'

Whenever there is a change of speaker, a new paragraph* is needed.

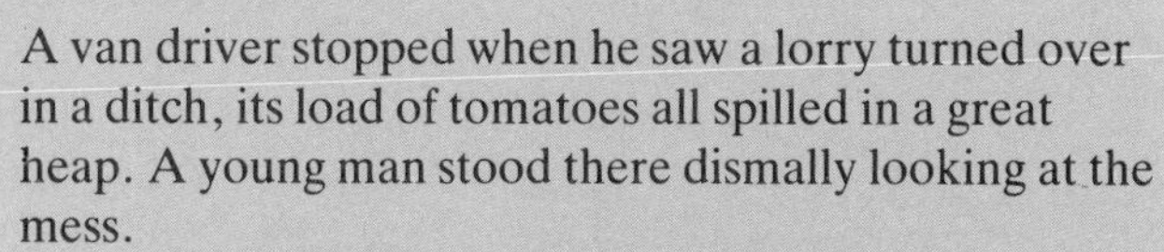

A van driver stopped when he saw a lorry turned over in a ditch, its load of tomatoes all spilled in a great heap. A young man stood there dismally looking at the mess.

'Come along,' the van driver said cheerfully. 'Let's go and get a cup of tea in the café over there. You'll feel better after that, and then I'll help you straighten out the lorry.'

'I don't think my father would like it,' said the young man.

'There's no need to worry about what your father would think,' said the van driver, and whisked him off to the café.

After they had drunk their tea, the young man said again, 'I still don't think my father's going to like this, you know.'

'Quit worrying about your father,' said the van driver. 'Where is your father, anyway?'

'He's under those tomatoes.'

doggerel

Verse that is too clumsy or too casually written to be called poetry is usually called doggerel. It is often meant to be amusing.

> Grandma, poor Grandma *is* in a fix;
> J. Paget, her grandson, is now all of six.
> Grandma, who really tries very hard,
> Can't think of a verse to write in his card.
> The words they all jumble – won't get into line.
> The full stops and commas all lag far behind,
> Determined to stop her from making a rhyme.
> So Grandma says, 'Bother! I'll just have to say,
> Our love to you, Joseph, on your 6th Birthday.'

double negative

A negative contradicts or says No.

They don't come here now.

They never come here now.

Both these sentences are negative, and mean much the same thing. But if we put them together, we make a double negative:

They don't never come here now.

This has quite a different meaning in standard English, because we have contradicted the 'never'. We have said 'not never', and if it is not never it must be sometimes. Colloquial* English isn't always as logical as that. If you say 'I don't have no tea', it's usually obvious from the context* and the way you say it (the intonation*), whether you mean the same as 'I have some tea', or the same as 'I don't have any tea'. In writing, it avoids confusion if you stick to standard English.

drama

This is another word for a 'play' – a story which is acted on the stage (or nowadays often in a television studio). The words of drama are to be spoken and are therefore direct speech*, but they are set out differently from direct speech in a novel. Instead of the unspoken words of ordinary reported speech, we have stage directions*.

emphatic pronouns

These are the same in form as reflexive pronouns*, but they are used for a different purpose. An emphatic pronoun underlines or emphasizes the person or thing referred to, eg

The captain *himself* is to blame for the team's failure.

We *ourselves* were not there when it happened.

Fortunately, the pavilion *itself* was not damaged by the boomerang.

English language

English has been in the making for many hundreds of years, and is still in the making today. When the Ancient Britons or Celts were driven out of England by the Angles and Saxons, they left only a few words behind them, including *clout, crock, dam, drudge, knob, mattock,* and *pool.* The Celtic language was almost entirely replaced by the language of the conquerors, now called Anglo-Saxon or Old English. It resembles English as we know it today, but only partly, because it has been changed and added to ever since.

Probably less than 30% of modern English derives from Old English. Many of the bricks from which modern English is built come from the Norman French, who conquered England in 1066. A lot of these French words in still earlier times came from Latin. And Latin also gave many words directly to the English language during the Renaissance (14th–16th centuries), when all serious education and writing was done in Latin, which was even spoken in English schools and universities.

If you think of modern English as a wall of language, it is built with a great variety of bricks. New bricks are always being added, and sometimes old bricks – old-fashioned words and phrases – fall off it too!

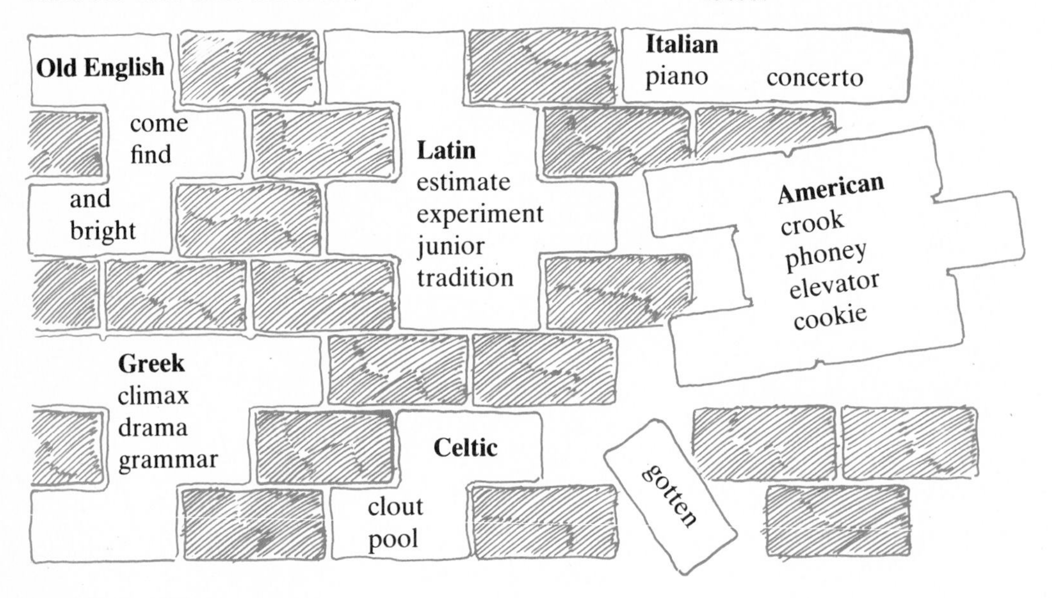

English place names

The names of places in England are of course all English now, but they came about in all sorts of ways and from all sorts of languages, just as the English language in general did. The name of London, for instance, was given by the Celts, who came to England about 500 BC.

The Romans occupied England from 43 AD to 450, when they were pushed out by the invading Angles and Saxons. They lived mostly in settlements or camps of their own and left such names as Doncaster (camp on the river Don) and Lancaster (camp on the river Lune).

The new invaders came to England in bands, each with its own leader. One such leader was Reada. His followers and dependents were called Readingas. The place where they finally settled came to be called Reading. They gave Knightsbridge its name because their knights (meaning 'young men' then) used to meet at the bridge.

By the time the Normans arrived in 1066, most places had been named, but they named a few places. Beaulieu (pronounced 'Bewley'), for example, was originally *beau lieu* meaning beautiful place, and Beaumont came from *beau mont* meaning beautiful hill.

Some places were named after famous people or saints, eg Cromwell, St Albans, St Helens. And some village names seem to have been invented by humorists, such as Snoring, Maggots End, Nicknocks and Nobottle.

envelopes

There are various ways of setting out the address* on an envelope. This page shows the most sensible and popular ways. In any case, you should always start the address about half way down the envelope, leaving at least 3.5 cm at the top for the stamp and postmark. You should also make sure the full address is given, including the post code if possible.

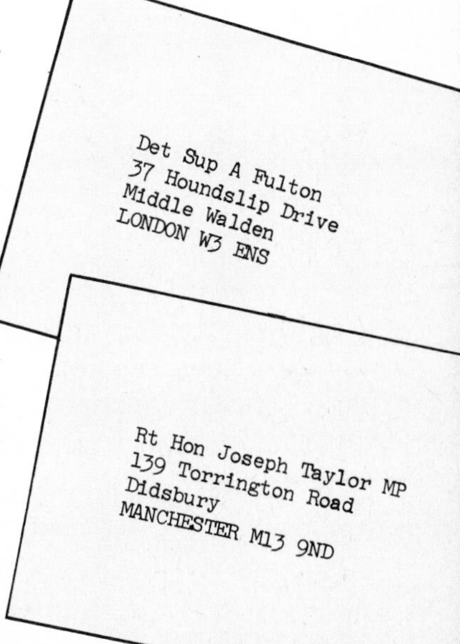

epitaphs

A short description of a dead person in prose or verse*, usually inscribed on a gravestone, is called an epitaph. They are normally very serious, and attempt to sum up a person's character and life.

> In loving memory of John Blank. He lived to the advantage of all around him, and died to the disadvantage of everyone.

Occasionally an epitaph would sum up the character of a villain. In St Paul's Church, in Covent Garden, London, there is this epitaph to Charles Duval, the French highwayman, who came to England during the Restoration (1600–1670) and became notorious as a robber and as a lady's man, being executed at Tyburn in 1670:

Here lies Duval; reader, if male thou art,
Look to thy purse; if female, to thy heart.

There also grew up a rather macabre custom of inventing humorous epitaphs, some written by well-known writers.

essays

A formal composition* in which you set down your ideas on a subject is called an essay. It is often used as a test of a person's writing ability, especially towards the end of secondary education and onwards. More loosely, any composition written in school is sometimes referred to as an essay.

A good essay is made up of several paragraphs* well knitted together by link words*. The first paragraph shows clearly what the subject is, and then each succeeding paragraph deals with one aspect only of the subject. With the final paragraph, the essay is rounded off by summing up or making some suitable comment on what you have said in order to show that a conclusion has been reached.

The essay that follows, taken and adapted from Richard Garrett's *The Story of Britain*, is a good example of a well-constructed essay. The opening sentence clearly states the subject. One aspect of human development is dealt with in each of the main paragraphs, and the final paragraph sums up the rest of the story. The paragraphs are tied together very simply with the link words 'these people' in the second paragraph, 'the first people' in the third, and 'these tools' in the last.

Half a million years ago, there were man-like creatures roaming the earth. They were probably able to make and use stone implements; they almost certainly knew how to build fires. Two hundred and fifty thousand years later, these ancestors of present day man had become more recognizably members of our own species. We know this from pieces of a human skull that were discovered in a quarry at Swanscombe in Kent one day in 1936.

How did these people from the early morning of history live? They moved from one forest clearing to the next; from one cave to another. Life was a never-ending search for food. They hunted the woolly rhino, the mastodon (a hairy elephant) and wild horses. For the rest of their diet, they lived off roots, berries and insects. By trial and error, they discovered what was poisonous, and what was not. When there was no other meat, they probably became cannibals.

The first people manufactured their weapons by chipping bits off large lumps of stone, or sharpening wooden stakes. In about 20,000 BC the last of the Ice Ages began to melt away, and by about 12,000 BC the ice had finally receded. People then learned to make better tools and weapons, using bones as well as flints.

As language developed, it helped men to co-operate in using these tools to chop down trees, clear spaces in the forests, and grow crops. They kept cattle, pigs and sheep. They dug mines from which to quarry flint. And they built homes, not unlike the huts in which some people still live today.

etymology

This is the study of the origin or derivation* of words. You can often guess the meaning of a word from its etymology. Take the word homophone*. It comes from two Greek words, *homo* ('the same') and *phonos* ('sound'). So homophones are words which sound the same.

euphemism

When we seek to hide the real nature of something unpleasant by wrapping it up in pleasant words, we are said to use a euphemism. Sometimes a euphemism can be justified, eg if you would otherwise hurt a person's feelings by being too blunt. There is, however, no point in keeping it up any longer than necessary. It is one thing to talk of a person 'passing away' when his relatives are still grieving, but silly two years later still to be saying 'he passed away'. 'He died' is much more direct and honest.

Euphemisms can be taken too far. Up to the close of the eighteenth century, the word 'belly' was perfectly respectable. Then 'refined' people began to think it was vulgar and used 'stomach' instead. Before long they decided that 'stomach' was a vulgar word too, and said 'tummy' instead. Now we are on our way back to accepting 'belly' as a good word!

For what direct words do you think these euphemisms stand?
perspire
expectorate
manure
supreme sacrifice
paying guest
senior citizen
To see a man about a dog
To spend a penny
Under the weather

exaggeration

Exaggeration may be used for emphasis. It then becomes figurative language* called hyperbole*:
I scored millions of goals last Sunday!

examples

When writing, we often need to make what we are saying clearer by giving an example of what is being described or explained, eg

> He was a boy of great determination. For example, when he made up his mind that he was going to be a good athlete, he went into training and devoted all his energies to it until he became the champion athlete of the school.

Here the example gives the boy's determination a clearer meaning. An example and an illustration* are much the same thing. Throughout this book an example is added wherever it will help to show more concretely what is meant. Sometimes it is introduced by 'eg', an abbreviation* meaning 'for example'.

exclamation marks

The exclamation mark (!) is the punctuation mark used after interjections*, eg Bother! Alas! Good gracious! Oh dear! It is also used to indicate any other exclamation* expressed as a full sentence, as in:
How beautifully she dances!
What a disagreeable fellow he is!
The exclamation mark is sometimes also used after a command to indicate an abrupt order:
Hurry up, Michael! Go away, you beast!
Notice that when an exclamation is set out as direct speech, the exclamation mark goes inside the quotation marks*, eg
'What a wonderful view!' exclaimed Jill.

exclamations

An exclamation is the name of a sentence which expresses feelings that come out with a rush, emphatic commands, or surprising information. The feeling of surprise, urgency, horror or whatever, is indicated by an exclamation mark*:

What an awful thing to say! How I hate you!
Danger! Keep out!

explanatory compositions

When we explain in some detail what, how or why something is, our explanation may be called an explanatory composition.

Like any good composition, an explanatory one should be divided into paragraphs*, have a clear introduction* and be woven together by link words*. A special concluding paragraph is not often needed in this sort of composition; it ends when the explanation is complete. Here is an explanation of why it rains.

Rain results from the rising and cooling of air. When air carrying invisible water vapour is cooled, the vapour condenses to form tiny droplets of water, so small that they float in the air and are visible as cloud or mist. As more vapour condenses, the cloud grows darker. When the droplets join together, they become heavier and fall – as rain.

How does the moving air get cooled? In general the temperature of the air falls as height increases. So if air is forced upwards, it cools.

Sometimes this is due to the shape of the land, for example when a range of hills forces the warm air upwards. Rain thus caused is called *orographic rain.* Again, when a mass of warm air meets a mass of cold air, the warm air (being less dense) floats upwards over the wedge of cold air. Rain caused by this is called *cyclonic rain.* Hotter areas of ground, such as towns, also warm the air and make it rise in 'convection currents', to cool and produce *convectional rain.*

fables

A short story told for the purpose of teaching a lesson is called a fable. The characters in most fables are animals, and they are often made to speak like humans. The fable of the tortoise and the hare, for example, teaches us that if we are slow but sure, we are more likely to be successful than if we are too hasty. The fable of the dog with the stolen meat and his reflection in the stream teaches us that the greedy may lose everything by wanting too much.

Looked at in another way, fables often give an illustration* of the truth of a well-known proverb*. The fable of the tortoise and the hare illustrates the proverb, 'Slow and steady wins the race'. The fable of the dog and his reflection illustrates the proverb, 'Grasp all; lose all'.

What proverb do you think the fable below illustrates? It is from Aesop's famous collection of fables, translated into modern English.

A crow was perched on one of the branches of a tall tree. There was a piece of meat in her beak. A hungry fox at that moment passed under the tree and saw the meat. It made his mouth water. He stopped and looked up at the crow.

'You are very beautiful,' he said in his politest voice. 'I wonder if your voice is as beautiful as you look.'

The crow felt very proud to be called beautiful and immediately wanted to show the fox how beautiful her voice was too. So she opened her beak wide and began to sing.

The meat of course fell out of her beak as she did so. It landed on the ground close to the fox, which was precisely what the cunning fox hoped would happen.

'Thank you,' he said to the crow, and ran off with the meat in his jaws.

What is the literal meaning of these idioms?

1. to spin a yarn
2. to turn an idea down
3. to run across someone
4. to clear the decks
5. to lend an ear
6. in the long run
7. a bolt from the blue
8. under one's breath

feminine gender

This term is used to refer to the pronouns *she*, *her*, *hers*. It is also still sometimes used to refer to nouns* naming female creatures, such as *cow* and *duck*, as opposed to the male creatures *bull* and *drake*. But there is really no such thing as gender* in English nouns, only the sex of the creatures named. The difference is explained in the entry on gender*.

figurative language

Any use of language that gives it a meaning different from its literal* meaning is said to be figurative. If you call a well-informed person a walking encyclopedia, you are using figurative language. The literal meaning of a walking encyclopedia is an encyclopedia that walks. You certainly don't mean that. You mean that the person has something like the knowledge contained in an encyclopedia but, unlike an encyclopedia, the person has legs.

'John is a walking encyclopedia' is a special form of figurative language called a metaphor*. Metaphors are the most common form of figurative language – so common that figurative language is often called metaphorical language.

If you say 'John is as knowledgeable as an encyclopedia', you are using a simile*. This is not quite as figurative as a metaphor. You are not saying that John *is* an encyclopedia, but merely that he is like one. Yet it is still far from literal, since John has no pages, no illustrated cover, and no printed words inside him!

Many idioms* are figurative too. Even a phrasal verb* like *ran up* in 'Diana ran up a dress in a couple of hours' is highly figurative. The literal meaning is very different!

first names

In a multi-racial society, where people are of various religions or none, the term Christian name is rightly going out of use, to be replaced by 'first name'.

How are English first names chosen? Parents may choose a name because it is uncommon, posh, biblical, traditional, pleasant-sounding; because a famous person had the name; because their best friend has; because it is a family name, or just because it is trendy. But for whatever reasons parents think they choose the name, there is usually some influence coming, however indirectly, from what other people are choosing.

For this reason a name may be very popular one year, only to be equally rare a few years later. In 1950, for example, the name Mark was so seldom chosen that it did not even appear in the first fifty most popular names. Yet by 1968 it was the most popular of all boys' names in England and Wales. It was very different in the 19th century, when William, John, George, Thomas, James and Henry were the six most popular boys' names year after year.

New first names have been added down the centuries. To the Old English Edwin, Egbert, Shirley, etc were added the Norman French names Guy, Richard, William, Louise, etc. To these were added biblical names such as John, Peter, James, Paul and Mary, and then Latin and Greek names, such as Diana, Cynthia, Sylvia, Alexander and Julius. The additions continued, eg Michelle (French), Leela (Indian), Ivan (Russian), Sarah (Hebrew).

In addition, some names have been derived from place names (Brent, Florence, Kent), from plants (Hazel, Heather, Violet), from months (April, May, June), from surnames (Warren, Percy, Lee, Douglas), and from literature

Abbreviated First Names	
Andy	(Andrew)
Cathy	(Catherine)
Chris	(Christine or Christopher)
Dick	(Richard)
Di	(Diana)
Geoff	(Geoffrey)
Jim	(James)
Jo	(Joanna)
Ken	(Kenneth)
Liz	(Elizabeth)
Mike	(Michael)
Pam	(Pamela)
Pat	(Patricia or Patrick)
Phil	(Philip)
Ron	(Ronald)
Sue	(Susan)
Tim	(Timothy)
Tom	(Thomas)
Val	(Valerie)
Vicky	(Victoria)

(Vanessa, Lorna, Wendy). One name that suddenly became popular was Tracey. It was first used by the actress Jean Simmons in 1956 in honour of Spencer Tracey. By 1964 it was the most popular of all girls' names, and remained so for a number of years.

I CAN SEE YOU; YOU ARE ME.

first person

The person who is speaking (the I or me) is referred to as the first person; the person spoken to (you) as the second person*; the person or thing spoken about (he, she, it, him, her) as the third person*. The first person therefore refers to the pronouns *I* and *me* and their plural* forms *we* and *us*. See also *person**.

foreign words and phrases

English speakers have always used words from other languages. If they have proved to be useful, they have in time become a part of the normal language, but naturally when they are first used they are regarded as foreign. Many foreign words are still in the process of becoming English. Until they are finally absorbed into the language, they often retain some sign of their foreign origins. The words *cliché, début, précis* retain their French accents, which are not a normal feature of English. The Latin *vide* and *viva voce* are still given their Latin pronunciation, as are the French *grand prix, à la carte, en route, hors d'oeuvre*.

Some words, mostly Latin, have long been part of the language but still show their origin by having foreign plurals.

Some Foreign Plurals
antenna – antennae
appendix – appendices
crisis – crises
fungus – fungi
larva – larvae
stimulus – stimuli
tableau – tableaux
terminus – termini

When foreign words, and especially foreign phrases, can make no claim to being part of the language, they are written in italics to show this.

circa (about)
modus operandi (way of working)
ex libris (from the library of)
schadenfreude (delight in others' misfortune)
tour de force (a feat of strength)

full stops

The full stop is the normal punctuation mark used to show that a sentence has been completed. But when the sentence is in the form of a question*, a question mark is used instead, and when it is in the form of an exclamation*, an exclamation mark is used. A full stop is thus used to end all statements* and normal commands*.

Today is the last day of the month.
Be careful not to touch the wet paint.

Notice that a full stop is used to end a sentence containing direct speech* even when the spoken sentence already ends with a question mark or exclamation mark.

'Will you let her take it?' asked John.
'Over my dead body!' exclaimed Steve.

If there is no question mark or exclamation mark after the 'sentence' within the sentence, a comma is used.

'That is not at all what I meant,' said Mike.

Another use of the full stop is to show that a word is an abbreviation*, eg Broad St. Nowadays there is a tendency to omit the full stop here, and after the initials used in abbreviations, eg BBC, GPO, BUPA, UN, though full stops are still normally used after the initials of a person's name, eg G.S.Fraser.

future tense

This is the tense* of the verb used to indicate that the action has still to happen in the future:

Tomorrow will be Thursday.
He will have finished it by the weekend.
The work will be done by Monday.

Notice however that in English the present tense, especially with *going to*, is often used instead of the future tense to express future action.

I am going to finish it tomorrow.
Tuesday is going to be the last day.
I'm coming home tomorrow.
I leave for Paris next Friday.

gender

In languages like Latin and French all nouns have gender. In French, for example, *la porte* (the door) is feminine, but *le feu* (the fire) is masculine, and this is shown by the different articles* (*la* and *le*). Gender therefore has nothing to do with sex. In Italian, for example, *un elephante* is masculine and *una giraffa* is feminine, no matter which sex the animal itself happens to be!

Gender does not apply to English nouns. Yet old-fashioned books still talk as if it did, because English grammar* was at first modelled on Latin, where all nouns have gender. There are, however, a few dozen nouns in English that have male and female versions, eg hero – heroine, lion – lioness, lad – lass, marquis – marchioness. But more frequently the males and females are called by entirely different nouns, eg cock – hen, duck – drake, bachelor – spinster.

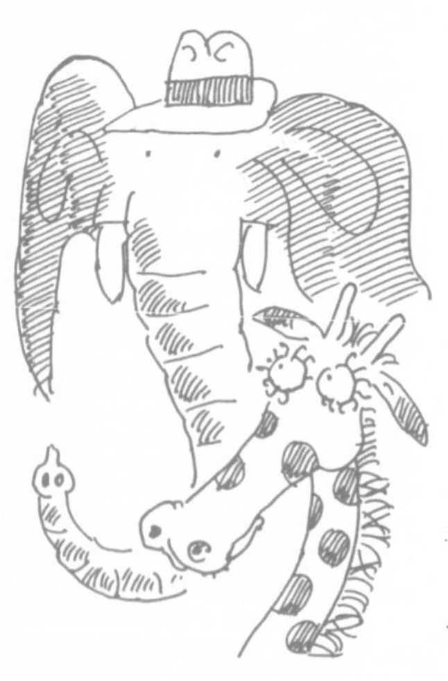

Just as there are no masculine or feminine nouns in English but only nouns naming male or female creatures, so there are no nouns of

Male	Female
actor	actress
boar	sow
bridegroom	bride
buck	doe
bull	cow
bullock	heifer
colt	filly
duke	duchess
earl	countess
emperor	empress
executor	executrix
gander	goose
god	goddess
host	hostess
husband	wife
king	queen
lord	lady
master	mistress
nephew	niece
prince	princess
ram	ewe
son	daughter
stallion	mare
uncle	aunt
waiter	waitress
widower	widow

common gender, but only nouns naming creatures whose sex is not indicated, such as person, child, parent, crocodile, sheep.

In the same way, there are no neuter* nouns but only nouns naming things that have no sex, such as hill, door, fire, football, pencil, water.

Gender does, however, apply to English pronouns: he, him (masculine), she, her (feminine), it (neuter). Some nouns are occasionally treated as if they had gender, such as a ship ('she's a lovely yacht').

generalisation

To generalise is to make a general statement to cover a number of particular facts, eg

They were often hungry or thirsty. They suffered from many diseases. Daytime was too hot and night-time too cold. Their work was burdensome and they always felt threatened.

These facts can be generalised by saying:

They suffered many hardships.

genitive case

The form of a noun or pronoun that shows possession is said to be the genitive or possessive* case, eg The *boy's* first words were: 'That is not my book; *mine* has a red cover.' The noun *boy's* and the pronoun *mine* both show possession and are in the possessive case. Nouns are made to show possession by means of the apostrophe*.

gerund

The noun formed from a verb and ending in *-ing* (not to be confused with the present participle*) is called a gerund or verbal noun.

Eating in a restaurant can be very enjoyable.
He likes *eating* in restaurants.
Let's celebrate by *eating* in a restaurant.

grammar

The word derives from a Greek word meaning the science of letters. Today it means the study of the way in which we use language in general. It therefore covers the whole use and form of words in sentences and includes spelling*, pronunciation, etymology*, inflexion*, word formation, the order of words in the sentence, agreement* of subject and verb, case*, tenses*, parts of speech*, clauses*, punctuation* and idioms*.

Grammar changes as language changes over the years. What is considered incorrect English or 'bad grammar' one year may be regarded as perfectly good grammar fifty years later. Not so many years ago teachers spent time pointing out that 'It's me' was bad grammar; it should be 'It's I'. Today 'It's me' is regarded as perfectly good grammar, while anyone who says 'It's I' would be thought hopelessly pedantic. In the same way, several generations ago, an educated person could (and did) say 'Ain't I invited too?' Today this is unacceptable – bad grammar. An educated person today says 'Aren't I invited too?' or more formally he might say 'Am I not invited too?'

greetings

The way you greet or address the person you are writing to is called a greeting or salutation. It generally begins with the polite 'Dear . . .'. But the exact form of the greeting will depend on the person you are writing to. If you are very friendly with the person, you can be quite informal. If you know the person reasonably well but he or she is distinctly your senior or superior, you will be more polite and formal. If you don't know the person at all, and especially if you are writing to an official, you will be completely formal:

Dear Jim, My dearest, Dear Smuts (informal)
Dear Mr Brown, Dear Aunt Jane (polite)
Dear Sir, Dear Madam, Dear Sirs (formal)

group names

This is another way of saying class names, which are discussed under classification*.

hackneyed phrases

A hackney was an overworked and very commonplace horse. A hackneyed phrase is thus one that is overused and stale. It should be avoided whenever you are writing carefully and want to appear at all original. It's another name for a cliché*.

head people

The head of an office is called a manager. The head of a prison is called a governor, and the head of the British Government is called the Prime Minister.

The group	The head
embassy	ambassador
committee	chairman
orchestra	conductor
destroyer	commander
lawcourt	magistrate
university	chancellor

What are the special names of the heads of the following?

1. a football team
2. a daily newspaper
3. a supermarket
4. a library
5. a regiment
6. a police force

homes

There are many special names for homes in English. The home of pigs is often a sty. A badger lives in a set, while squirrels build a drey for their home. A non-conformist minister usually calls his home a manse, but the vicar of a Church of England parish lives in a vicarage.

Tenant	Home
beaver	lodge
bishop	palace
convict	prison
dog	kennel
horse	stable
lion	den
otter	holt
sheep	fold
tiger	lair

Whose homes are called by these names?

1. a hive
2. a caravan
3. an earth
4. a hutch
5. a burrow
6. a lodge
7. a monastery
8. a tent
9. an eyrie

homonyms

This term derives from two Greek words meaning 'the same' and 'name'. Homonyms are therefore words that are spelt alike but have different meanings.

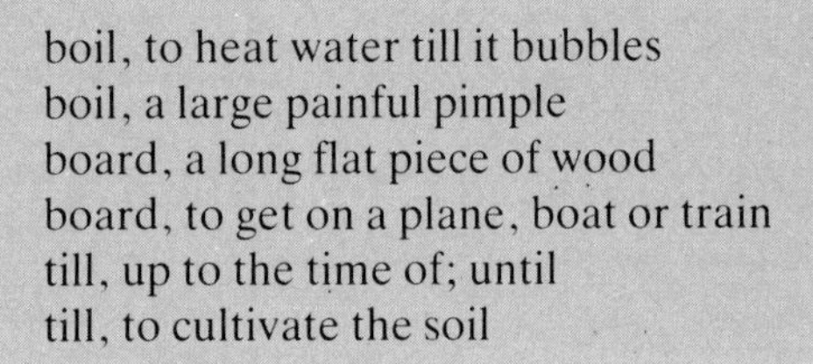

boil, to heat water till it bubbles
boil, a large painful pimple
board, a long flat piece of wood
board, to get on a plane, boat or train
till, up to the time of; until
till, to cultivate the soil

homophones

This term comes from two Greek words meaning 'the same' and 'sound'. Homophones therefore sound alike but have different spellings.

beer, an alcoholic drink
bier, a frame for carrying a coffin
fair, a market or a fun place
fare, the price paid for a journey
meat, the flesh of animals used for eating
meet, to encounter
phrase, a group of words functioning as a unit
frays, fights
right, correct
write, to set down on paper
wait, to stay for something
weight, heaviness

Homophones can cause difficulty with spelling: which meaning has which spelling? When used orally, they can cause confusion about what is meant. This oral confusion can be deliberately used as a joke, called a pun* (which is much funnier when spoken than when written down).

> Four drinking companions carried the bier at this drunkard's funeral.

Some More Homophones
air – heir
bail – bale
ball – bawl
bare – bear
berth – birth
bough – bow
boy – buoy
ceiling – sealing
cereal – serial
currant – current
die – dye
faint – feint
foul – fowl
groan – grown
hair – hare
heard – herd
hole – whole
knows – nose
lessen – lesson
missed – mist
one – won
road – rode

humour

Humour is the quality of a situation or happening that makes you laugh or smile. A person with a good sense of humour quickly appreciates this funny side of things. There should clearly be humour in any use of English that is meant to be funny, such as jokes*, puns*, riddles*, limericks*, schoolboy howlers*, nonsense verse*. Humour and wit are similar, but wit is more clever and less sympathetic as in the joke below.

> The Greens had invited the Smithsons to dinner and while they were preparing the meal they asked their daughter to entertain the guests.
>
> 'Not very p-r-e-t-t-y is she?' said Mr Smithson to his wife.
>
> 'No,' said the little girl, 'but she's very b-r-i-g-h-t.'

hyperbole

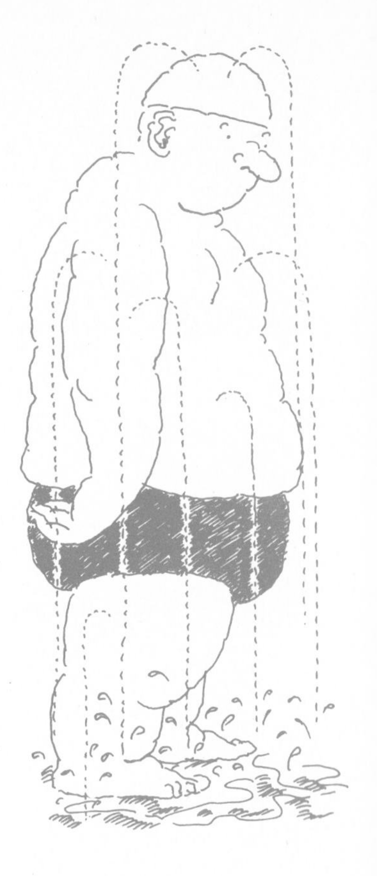

When we exaggerate, not to deceive but to emphasize what we are saying, or even to produce a humorous effect, we use the kind of figurative language* that is called hyperbole, eg After my swimming lesson there was more water inside me than in the swimming pool.

hyphen

This punctuation mark (-) is used:

1. To join two or more words to make a single compound* word: easy-going, blood-red, governor-general.
2. To link words in certain place names: Southend-on-Sea, Ashby-de-la-Zouch.
3. After the prefix re- in certain words to avoid confusing them with their homonyms:
   re-bound, bound again
   rebound, to bounce back
   re-counted, counted again
   recounted, told.
4. To avoid the misleading appearance of a double *e* or a double *o* in such words as: co-operative, co-ordinated, re-echo, re-enter.
5. To indicate, when a word is broken at the end of a line, that the rest of the word is at the beginning of the next line. The breaks should not be haphazardly made, but made at the end of a syllable*:

wrong	*right*
hig-hest	high-est
pai-nful	pain-ful
telep-hone	tele-phone
pu-zzling	puz-zling

6. To avoid giving the wrong impression:
   Ten-pound notes, please.
   Ten pound notes, please.

idiomatic expressions

Strictly speaking, an idiom is any expression that is peculiar to a language. More generally, an idiomatic expression is any group of words that cannot be understood simply from the separate words that make up the group. Even a commonplace expression like *there are* is idiomatic when it does not literally mean *there* plus *are*.

There are seven days in a week. (idiomatic)

There are my shoes, over there. (literal)

Highly figurative idiomatic expressions are more obvious. If I say that John got into hot water, I clearly don't mean literally that he immersed himself in hot water and scalded himself. I mean that he was in trouble. Here are some more idiomatic expressions and their literal meanings:

What is the literal meaning of these expressions?
1. not up to the mark
2. to face the music
3. to sit on the fence
4. to make a mountain out of a molehill
5. a rough diamond
6. to be under a cloud
7. to hang one's head
8. to give someone the cold shoulder

to pull up short: to stop suddenly
to lead him up the garden path: to deceive him
to play the game: to act fairly
to hold one's tongue: to keep silent
to turn over a new leaf: to behave better
to play fast and loose: to act irresponsibly
to turn the tables: to reverse the result
forty winks: a short sleep
on all fours: on hands and knees
back to the wall: in great difficulty
a storm in a teacup: a lot of fuss about nothing
as the crow flies: in a straight line
by hook or by crook: by any means
on the square: honest
at a loose end: with nothing to do

‘if’ sentences

These are used to say that one thing depends on another, eg

If you dropped that glass, it would break.
I always walk to school if it is fine.

Tenses* formed with *would* are called conditional tenses (would break, would have broken, etc). Sometimes they are accompanied by verbs with the old subjunctive form (expressing doubt), eg If I *were* you, I would . . ., but most people now simply say: If I *was* you, I would . . .

illustrations

Just as an explanation can be made clearer or more concrete by an illustration in picture form, so can it be made clearer by an illustration or example* in word form. To illustrate means to throw light on something. The following sentence contains two illustrations of the generalisation* that Liz ‘belittled’ what Steve had been through.

> Liz belittled what Steve had been through, making light of his lack of food and laughing away the hardships of marching across the desert.

imperative

The imperative form of the verb is used to express commands*, prohibitions and requests. It takes the same form as the infinitive* without the ‘to’, eg

Stop quarrelling, you two. (command)
Please *open* the window. (request)
Don’t *leave* your calculator there. (prohibition)

incomplete verbs

Certain verbs that need a complement* to complete them are called incomplete verbs. The main ones are: to be, to become, to appear, to seem, to look. The complement is usually a noun or an adjective or one of their equivalents.

John *has become* captain of the team. (noun)
You *look* pale. (adjective)
Paddy *seems* in a hurry. (adjective phrase)

Other verbs such as get, grow, taste, smell, feel, turn, turn out, go, wear, make, prove, and come, can also be used as incomplete verbs.

Paddy *feels* ill. (adjective)
John *proved* a friend indeed. (noun)

indefinite article

The article* (*a* or *an*) used to refer to any one of a group of things is called the indefinite article.

A ladybird is *an* insect.

index

A reference book* is not much use if you do not know which page to turn to, to find the information you need. It's not always possible to have everything in alphabetical order. The problem is then solved by having an index. This is an alphabetical list at the back of the book of all the subjects, people and places dealt with or mentioned in the book. The more the subject matter is broken down, the better the index is. A book on football, for instance, might not only list *referee* as a subject but also aspects of the subject, usually as sub-headings after the main entry.

referee, authority of 106
dress 107
how appointed 197
penalising players 109
qualifications 106
quarrelling with 109

indirect speech

When someone reports what was said instead of giving the actual words spoken (direct speech*), we call it indirect or reported speech. The following examples show how direct speech becomes or is changed into indirect speech.

'I am going home,' said Diana.

'You haven't danced with me once this evening, Diana.' said Tom.

'Where have you put my shoes, Barbara?' asked John.

Diana said that she was going home.

Tom complained to Diana that she had not danced with him that evening.

John asked his girlfriend where she had put his shoes.

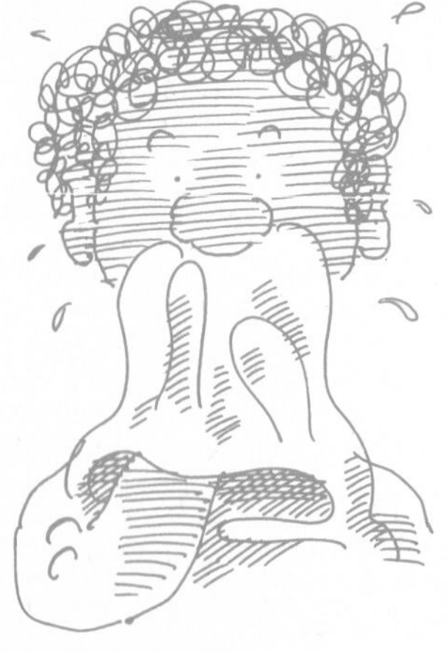

Can you report what these people said?

1. 'Paddy is my best friend,' said John.
2. 'I have a bad cold, Tom, so I can't come to your party,' said Paddy.
3. 'When will my records be returned, Steve?' asked Liz.
4. 'Go and get your hair cut, Steve,' said his mother.

infinitives

The infinitive is the simplest form of the verb*. It is the form given in dictionary entries. If you want to look up *counterfeiting*, for example, you will have to look up *counterfeit*, since that is the infinitive of the verb. Here are some past tense forms of verbs with their infinitives in brackets:

walked (walk)	shone (shine)
wobbled (wobble)	went (go)

The infinitive usually takes 'to', but not always: Will you help me *do* this? Where it does take 'to', the 'to' normally goes right in front of the infinitive, eg I need *to get* some money quickly, NOT I need *to quickly get* some money (this is called a *split infinitive*).

'No, you can't come in for coffee, Steve,' said Liz.

Liz told Steve that he could not come in for coffee.

inflexion

Any variation in the form of words to indicate a change of meaning or grammatical function is called inflexion. Old English was a highly inflected language, but over the centuries most of the inflexions have gradually disappeared, making modern English much simpler. Here are some examples of the few inflexions that remain in the language:

boy – boys, bush – bushes, knife – knives (plurals*)
John – John's, the girls – the girls' (genitive*)
big – bigger, able – abler (comparative*)
big – biggest, able – ablest (superlative*)
walk, walks, walking, walked (tenses*)

initials

Instead of giving a person's full name, the first letters of the names are often used for the sake of brevity. It is usual to show that they are initials by placing a full stop after each initial: A.J.Thompson (Anthony John Thompson).

inscriptions

Any message or record formally inscribed on stone, wood, a plaque or a book may be called an inscription. Book inscriptions* to discourage theft used to be popular. Today the inscription in a book is more likely to be from the giver to the receiver. Epitaphs* are a kind of inscription.

interjections

The interjection is the part of speech* which expresses an exclamation*. Interjections may express almost any strong feelings – surprise, regret, anger, approval, fear, disgust, disbelief or joy.

Oh! Damn! Whew! Impossible!
Alas! Great! Ugh! Hurrah!

The word *interjection* comes from the Latin meaning thrown into or inserted. Interjections are inserted into sentences; they do not form part of the normal plan of sentences. Their separation from the plan of the sentence is clear because they are usually followed by an exclamation mark*, as here:

'Great! That's a marvellous idea,' said Barbara.

When they don't have an exclamation mark (usually in the middle of a sentence), their separateness from the sentence plan is shown by commas, as here:

The rain, alas, continued all day.

Sometimes an interjection contains more than one word:

Goodness me! O dear!
Upon my soul! Well I never!

international languages

It has always been difficult for the people of the world to communicate with one another, as there are hundreds of different languages. During the 14th, 15th and 16th centuries Latin was spoken by most educated people all over the world, and Latin then served as the international language. As time went on, more and more people became educated but an ever smaller proportion of them spoke Latin. A new international language was needed.

As France was the most cultured country, French tended to be used as an international language in higher society. But as Britain was prosperous and powerful, English was also used internationally, especially in industry and commerce. Some other nations objected to a particular nation's language being used internationally. It was felt that there ought to be a language that everyone could use, not tied to any one nation.

This is an example of Esperanto.
Do you know what it says?
Por esti sukcesa politikisto, oni
ne devas esti pigra.

Several languages were 'invented' for this purpose, the most popular being Esperanto. Yet they were never very widely adopted, largely because English became rapidly more widely used as the result of America growing so rich and powerful. Eventually English became so common that, regardless of its origin, most countries accepted it as the international language. So today a Norwegian will write to a Chinese in English, and a Malay uses English to talk to a Belgian.

interrogative pronouns

These are the kind of pronoun* used to ask a question*: what, which, who, whom, whose? Here are examples of them at work, with the noun* they stand for in brackets:

Who won the race? (which competitor)
What did he do then? (what action)
Whose is this pen? (which person's)
Whom did you see? (which person)
Which did you choose? (which prize)

WHICH PRIZE DID SHE WIN?

intonation

The rise and fall of the voice when speaking is called intonation. It is an important means of making your meaning clear in conversation. The same sentence spoken with different intonation can mean two quite different things. Say these sentences aloud: I can begin now. I can begin now?

The first sentence is spoken with a falling intonation and means that you are ready to begin. The second is spoken with a rising intonation and asks if you are allowed to begin now.

intransitive verbs

See transitive verbs*

JOHN, MEET MY FRIEND, DEREK.

introductions

There are two main kinds of introduction: introducing one person to another, and introducing a subject at the beginning of a composition.

The first kind of introduction plays an important part in oiling the wheels of social life. It is usual to speak first to the person to whom you are introducing someone, like this:

> *You* John, I should like you to meet my friend Derek Taylor. Derek, this is John Kitson.
> *John* Hello, Derek. How do you do.
> *Derek* How do you do, John. I've heard a lot about you from Tom. It's good to meet you at last!

Friends should be introduced to parents in much the same way:

> *Teresa* Mum, meet my new friend Diana Kitson. Di, this is my mother.
> *Mrs Brown* Hello Diana – come on in!
> *Diana* Thank you, Mrs Brown.

Introductions to compositions take the form of a paragraph that clearly says what the composition is about. Sometimes this introductory paragraph will also deal with the first topic or point in the composition. Examples will be found under descriptions*, essays*, explanatory composition*, and narrative composition*.

A single paragraph may also have an introduction with a topic sentence*, which indicates what the paragraph is about, at the beginning. The topic sentence may, however, come last in the paragraph, to keep the reader keyed up to discover what it is all about. It then usually sums up what has been said.

inversion

The normal order of words in English is subject* followed by verb*: The children had never met such an oddity. The subject (the children) is followed by the verb (had met). But for the purpose of emphasis, the 'never' may be placed

NEVER HAD SHE BEEN SO SCARED

first: Never had the children met such an oddity.

The subject noun (children) now follows the auxiliary verb* (had). This is called an inversion. This kind of inversion can take place with negative adverbs like never, hardly, rarely, seldom, scarcely, only. It can also take place with phrases containing a negative adverb, such as almost never, exceedingly rarely, only once in her life, scarcely more than a moment: Only once in her life had she been as frightened as she was then.

Other adverbs or adverb phrases can sometimes be placed before the verb in order to emphasize them: Down came the rain. Along the narrow ledge he crept.

inverted commas

These punctuation marks are used to open or close a quotation, which is why they are also called quotation marks*. They used always to be in pairs, like this:

"He went that way," shouted John.

But single inverted commas are becoming usual, eg

'He must be hiding somewhere,' whispered Tom.

invitations

The most common kind is a friend's invitation to his or her party. These invitations are usually quite informal letters.

A less personal, but popular way of sending out an invitation is by means of a partly printed card. In either case, politeness requires a reply so that your friend will know exactly how many people are coming. The RSVP on the card means 'please reply'. People used to reply to formal invitations in the third person.

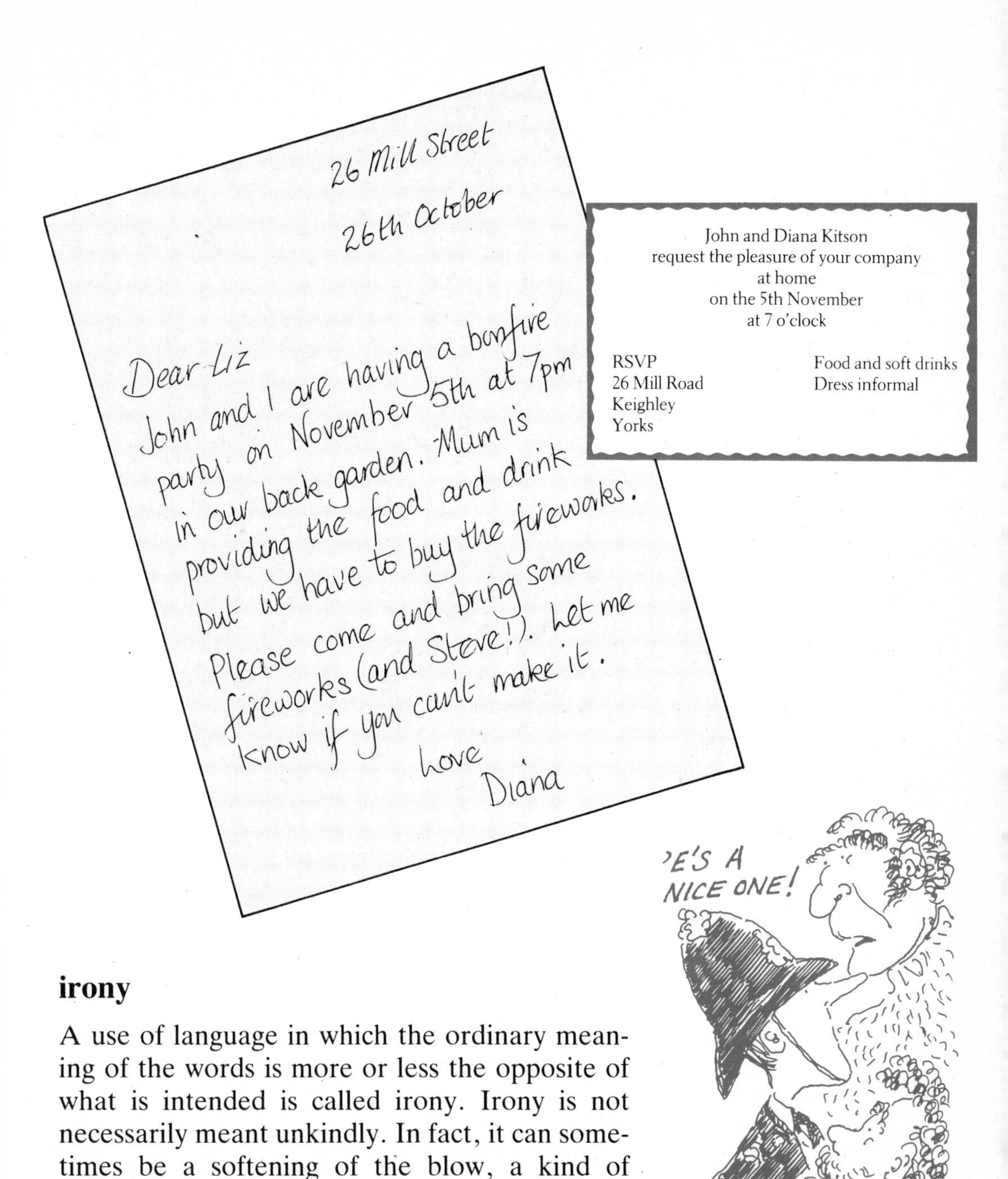

26 Mill Street

26th October

Dear Liz

John and I are having a bonfire party on November 5th at 7pm in our back garden. Mum is providing the food and drink but we have to buy the fireworks. Please come and bring some fireworks (and Steve!). Let me know if you can't make it.

Love

Diana

John and Diana Kitson
request the pleasure of your company
at home
on the 5th November
at 7 o'clock

RSVP
26 Mill Road
Keighley
Yorks

Food and soft drinks
Dress informal

irony

A use of language in which the ordinary meaning of the words is more or less the opposite of what is intended is called irony. Irony is not necessarily meant unkindly. In fact, it can sometimes be a softening of the blow, a kind of euphemism*. If you have done something unpleasant, for example, and instead of calling you an insufferable beast your friend says ironically 'You're a nice one!', your friend is using irony to criticise you in a friendly way.

When irony is used with the intention of wounding, it is called sarcasm*. If someone dropped a plate, for instance, and you said angrily, 'Go on, break all the crockery in the house; we shall be only too grateful!' you would be using sarcasm.

When you use irony, it is as if you were adding 'I don't think' after the remark, eg 'It's a pleasant occupation having teeth extracted, I don't think.'

irregular verbs

Regular verbs form their past tense* and their past participle* by adding -ed to the infinitive*, like this: to walk, I walked, I have walked.

But some 200 verbs behave differently. They make their past tense and/or past participle by a vowel change in the stem of the word, or by adding -en to the infinitive to make the past participle.

Some Irregular Verbs

to become, I became, I have become
to begin, I began, I have begun
to bite, I bit, I have bitten
to buy, I bought, I have bought
to creep, I crept, I have crept
to do, I did, I have done
to draw, I drew, I have drawn
to eat, I ate, I have eaten
to fall, I fell, I have fallen
to fight, I fought, I have fought
to give, I gave, I have given
to go, I went, I have gone
to hide, I hid, I have hidden
to kneel, I knelt, I have knelt
to know, I knew, I have known
to lay, I laid, I have laid
to lie, I lied, I have lied
to lie (down), I lay, I have lain
to ride, I rode, I have ridden
to ring, I rang, I have rung
to run, I ran, I have run
to see, I saw, I have seen
to shake, I shook, I have shaken
to sink, I sank, I have sunk
to spring, I sprang, I have sprung
to take, I took, I have taken

italics

This kind of printing uses sloping letters when in writing by hand we would underline the words – for emphasis, for foreign words, for titles, or for talking about a word as a word.

> I *do* wish you would drive more slowly.
> John made something of a *faux pas* by arriving half an hour late.
> He was reading a book called *The Death of a Hero*.
> The second *that* is not needed in that sentence.

jargon

Special language used only by a group of people – belonging, perhaps, to a particular religion, trade, profession, political party, club or society – is called jargon. It is full of the technical terms used by that group alone. It's a useful sort of shorthand within the group, but obviously to be avoided when speaking to outsiders – they won't know what you're talking about!

joining sentences

There are four main ways of joining two sentences to make a single sentence:

1. By means of conjunctions*:
   I missed the train. I stopped to chat.
   = I missed the train *because* I stopped to chat.
2. By means of relative pronouns*:
   The book is by Conrad. Tom is reading it.
   = The book *that* Tom is reading is by Conrad.
3. By means of a present participle*:
   Angus was coming home. He saw an elephant.
   = Coming home, Angus saw an elephant.
4. By means of a past participle*:
   We were beaten in the first match. We turned the tables in the second. = Beaten in the first match, we turned the tables in the second.

I eat my peas with honey;
I've done it all my life.
It makes the peas taste funny,
But it keeps them on the knife.

Timothy Jones
Liked a dinner of bones,
And for tea he would choose
A pair of old shoes.

His teeth grew so long,
So sharp and so strong,
That he bit off his face,
Leaving only a space.

joke poems

Any light verse that is mainly intended to be funny may be called a joke poem. The most popular form of joke poem is the limerick*. Most joke poems (like the one about the peas) are old and anonymous, but some authors are always writing new joke poems – like this one about Timothy Jones, by Ruth Ainsworth.

Sometimes the joke of a humorous poem may have a darker or crueller side. This one, for example, is a sick joke*:

> An accident happened to my brother Jim
> When somebody threw some tomatoes at him.
> Tomatoes are juicy and don't hurt the skin,
> But these had been carefully packed in a tin.

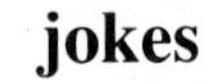

jokes

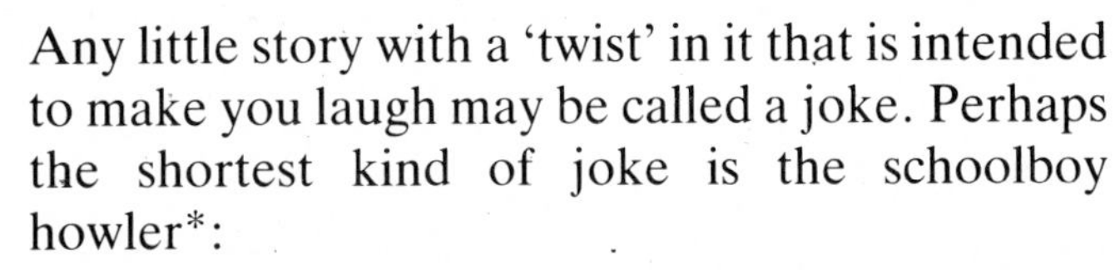

Any little story with a 'twist' in it that is intended to make you laugh may be called a joke. Perhaps the shortest kind of joke is the schoolboy howler*:

> A giraffe needs a long neck because its head is so far from its body.

Riddles* are usually meant to make you laugh, and are almost equally brief:

> Why do some people press a door bell with their finger, and others with their thumb?
> To get someone to open the door!

Jokes longer than these, however, usually contain dialogue* and should be set out with inverted commas*, starting a fresh line for every change of speaker.

> An old lady broke her leg. The doctor put plaster on it and told her she would not be able to go upstairs for several months, until he had removed it. At last he came to take it off.
>
> 'May I go up the stairs now?' asked the old lady.
>
> 'Yes you may,' the doctor replied.
>
> 'What a relief,' the old lady sighed. 'You've no idea how hard it's been to shin up the drain pipe at bedtime.'

lampoons

A lampoon is a comic verse* intended to make fun of someone in a hurtful way. The following lampoon, in the form of an epitaph*, is supposed to have been pinned on the door of King Charles II's bedroom:

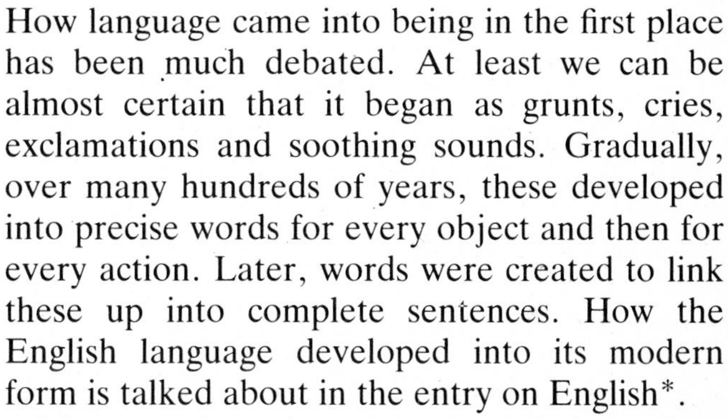

Here lies our Sovereign Lord, the King,
  Whose word no man relies on.
He never says a foolish thing,
  Nor ever does a wise one.

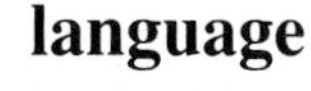

language

How language came into being in the first place has been much debated. At least we can be almost certain that it began as grunts, cries, exclamations and soothing sounds. Gradually, over many hundreds of years, these developed into precise words for every object and then for every action. Later, words were created to link these up into complete sentences. How the English language developed into its modern form is talked about in the entry on English*.

Man may have learnt to speak in one place and then carried language all over the world, or perhaps language was 'invented' in many different places. At any rate, whenever a large group of people formed a civilization of their own cut off from the rest of mankind, they developed a language of their own. In the end there were many completely different languages. English has become far and away the most widely used international language, though more people speak Chinese and Hindi than English as their first language (see the bar chart on the next page).

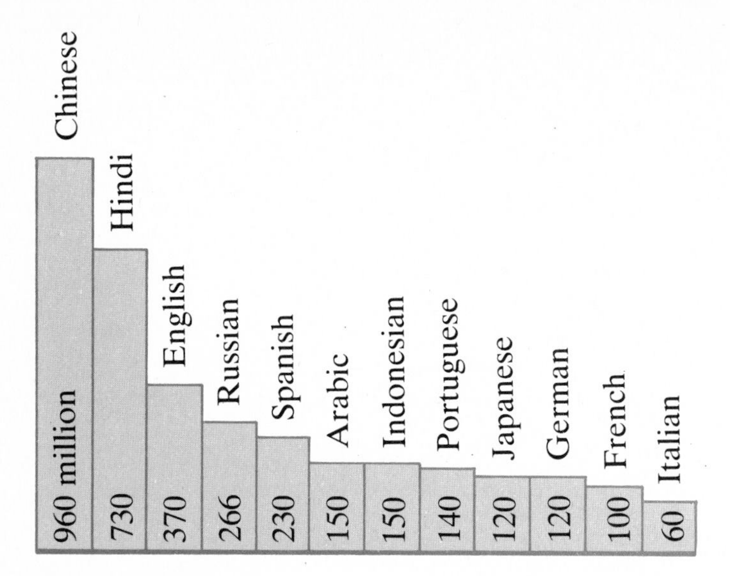

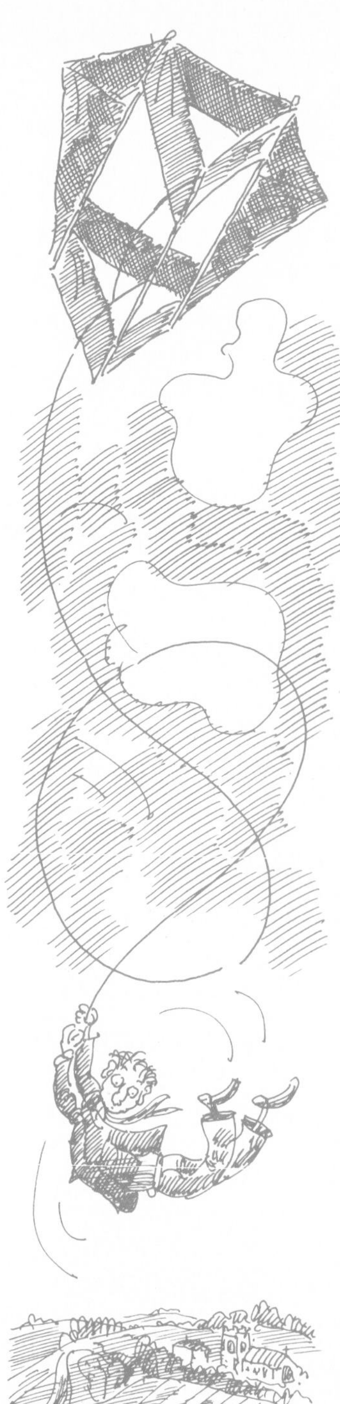

Latin derivations

A great many English words come from, or have a derivation* in Latin. For example, *navis* (a ship) gives us words such as navy, naval, navigator, and navigable. *Amo* (I love) gives us words such as amiable, amicable, and amateur.

letter writing

See business letters*, invitations*, personal letters*, and thank-you letters*.

limericks

A limerick is a kind of humorous poem. It always has five lines, or four if you run the third and fourth lines together. You can recognize it immediately by its beat and rhymes. Here are some examples:

A daring young fellow called Knight
Was flying a very large kite;
  But the wind was too strong
  And he held on too long,
And soon he was quite out of sight.

There was a young man of Bengal
Who went to a fancy dress ball.
He went, just for fun,
Dressed up as a bun –
A dog ate him up in the hall!

Most limericks are anonymous. That is to say, we no longer know who made them up. But we do know one man who wrote a lot of limericks, and first made the limerick so popular: the nonsense* poet and painter, Edward Lear. His limericks are slightly different from the limerick form that is commonest today. The last word is usually the same as the end word of the first line, as you can see from this example:

There was an old man with a beard,
Who said, 'It is just as I feared!
Two Owls and a Hen,
Four Larks and a Wren,
Have all built their nests in my beard!'

Can you make up some limericks? It's quite easy when you know how to put them together. The first, second and last lines always rhyme with each other; so do the third and fourth lines. Check this on the examples above. You'll notice, too, that the third and fourth lines are shorter than the others.

links

Although the sentence* is a complete unit of language ending with a full stop, it is not independent of other sentences in a continuous piece of writing. The sentences have to follow on naturally and smoothly; they have to show how the next thought is added on to the one before. Sometimes the connection doesn't need to be shown because there is an obvious logical or time sequence.

> The lion crept towards its prey. The deer went on drinking. The lion crept a little nearer. The deer lifted its head alertly. With one bound the lion hurled itself towards the deer . . .

But more often the link between one sentence and the next has to be definitely suggested in order to make the meaning clear.

> All cowboys had to be good horsemen. This was because they lived in the saddle. Almost every cowboy owned a horse. Some even owned a spare one. But on the ranch they might have the use of five or six more horses. These mounts belonged to the ranch owner.

The word *This* links the second sentence to the first. *Almost every cowboy* loosely links the third to the first two. *Some even owned* links immediately with the previous sentence. The link word in the next sentence is *But* to show the contrast between owning one or two horses and having the use of five or six. Finally, *These* in the last sentence links directly with 'five or six horses' in the sentence before.

Links between paragraphs* are just as important. The reader needs to know what the connection between the topic of one paragraph and

the next is; otherwise he will not be able to follow the composition* at all easily. Notice the links between the four paragraphs of the composition about salmon migration.

The Migration of the Salmon

Some fish spend all their life in the place where they were born. Salmon do not. They migrate back and forth between the ocean and the river.

They leave the ocean in the autumn and travel far up the river. They have to fight against the current and even jump up waterfalls. Sometimes they travel for 2000 miles before they spawn.

Year after year the salmon go back up the river to spawn where they were hatched. The female fish makes a nest in the sand at the bottom of the river by flapping the sand with her tail. She lays her eggs in the nest, and the male salmon leaves his sperm to fertilize the eggs. Then the female salmon covers the nest with sand, and leaves them to hatch on their own.

Not till the winter do the young fish hatch out. When they are a few inches long, they swim backwards down the river. They are really carried down by the current. When they reach the open sea, they are big enough to turn round and face the world under water head-on. Then next autumn they will return far up the same river where they were hatched, and the sequence will be repeated.

The link words in the second paragraph are *They leave the ocean*. They link the new paragraph to the first one by telling us how the salmon are connected with the ocean mentioned in the first paragraph. *Go back to spawn* in the third paragraph shows clearly that the paragraph is going to say more about the topic of spawning mentioned in the last sentence of the second paragraph. Then the last sentence of the third paragraph talks of leaving the eggs to hatch out; so *the young fish hatch out* in the last paragraph follows on from this, making a natural link.

literal language

This is language used in its most straightforward sense, not with an underlying meaning. Literal language can be taken to mean what it says, word for word. It is the opposite of figurative language*, which cannot be taken word for word because it has an underlying meaning. For example, when we talk of the camel being the ship of the desert, *ship of the desert* is figurative language, not literal, since the camel is not literally a ship, nor does it sail on the desert. The underlying meaning is that the camel is very good for transport in the desert.

malapropisms

A ludicrous misuse of a word, especially in mistake for one resembling it, is call a malapropism after Mrs Malaprop in Sheridan's play *The Rivals*. If, for example, you say that pythons are an eyesore in the landscape, when you really mean 'pylons', you are uttering a malapropism.

masculine gender

In English the masculine gender* survives only in the personal pronouns* *he* and *him*, and in the possessive pronoun* *his*. English nouns do not have gender; there are merely some nouns, such as *stallion* or *colt*, that name male creatures. The difference is explained in the entry on gender*.

messages

Practically everyone has to deliver a message from time to time. The words you use in delivering the message are of course different from those used by the sender, eg:

Mrs Kitson John, go and tell Mrs Taylor she's welcome to watch our new video.

John Good morning, Mrs Taylor. Mum says you're welcome to watch our new video.

metaphors

Sometimes, for the sake of emphasis or vividness, we speak of a thing or an action as if it actually were something which it really only resembles. This figurative* (not literal*) use of language is called metaphor.

My sister Jenny is a pig.

The sergeant barked out his orders.

Mr Lee shook my hand with a grip of iron.

Jenny isn't really a pig; the sergeant didn't really bark in the same way as a dog or a seal, because he spoke words; and, unless Mr Lee has a mechanical limb, the third example is metaphorical too.

Middle English

The state English had reached by the Middle Ages, after it had absorbed most of the borrowings from Norman French, is called Middle English. It is recognizably like modern English, as can be seen from *The Canterbury Tales* by Geoffrey Chaucer (1340–1400).

Whan that Aprill with his shoures soote
The droghte of March hath perced to the roote,
And bathed every veyne in swich licour
Of which vertu engendred is the flour;
Whan Zephirus eek with his sweete breeth 5
Inspired hath in every holt and heeth
The tendre croppes, and the yonge sonne
Hath in the Ram his halve cours yronne,
And smale foweles maken melodye,
That slepen al the nyght with open ye 10
(So priketh hem nature in hir corages);
Thanne longen folk to goon on pilgrimages,
And palmeres for to seken straunge strondes,
To ferne halwes, kowthe in sondry londes;
And specially from every shires ende 15
Of Engelond to Caunterbury they wende,
The hooly blisful martir for to seke,
That hem hath holpen whan that they were seeke.

middle names

Most children are given two names before their surname in Britain (and a few have three or four). The second of these is called the middle name. Nearly all Americans keep their middle name or at least the initial even in their signature, eg Robert J. Wilson, Daphne N. Heydrick.

Many English first names* were originally surnames. A child might be given its mother's surname as a middle name; since middle names weren't much used anyway, it didn't matter that it was normally a surname. Then, gradually, people began to use these middle names – names such as Percy, Douglas, Clifford or Warren – as first names.

misused words

Some words have so often been misused that the way or sense in which they were misused has become accepted English. The adjective *awful* used to mean full of awe. It was so often misused to mean very bad that it has now changed its meaning accordingly. Older people tend to resent these changes. At present, for example, different *to* is accepted, though it used to be only different *from*, but different *than* is not accepted and is still regarded in Britain as a misuse of English.

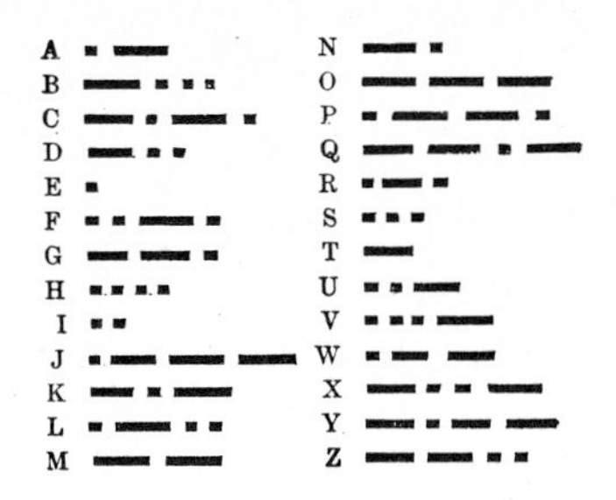

morse code

This is a signalling code* invented by Sam Morse (1791–1872), in which letters or numbers are made up of dots and dashes, long and short flashes, or long and short sounds. The complete Morse alphabet is shown here – try using it for some messages of your own.

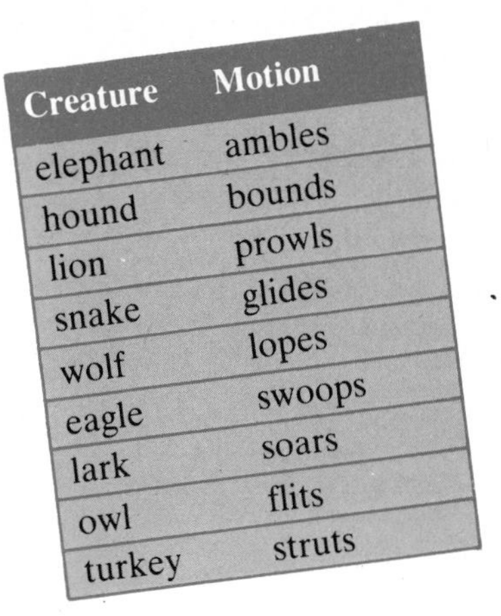

Creature	Motion
elephant	ambles
hound	bounds
lion	prowls
snake	glides
wolf	lopes
eagle	swoops
lark	soars
owl	flits
turkey	struts

motion

Creatures do not just move; they move in particular ways, and the verb* which expresses that motion is different in each case: A bear for example *ambles*; a donkey often *trots*; a mouse *scampers*; a duck *waddles*; an old man *totters*.

Inanimate objects have special ways of moving too: A sluggish river *meanders*; leaves *flutter* in the breeze; a stream *trickles*; the rain *pours*; smoke *drifts*; doors *slam*.

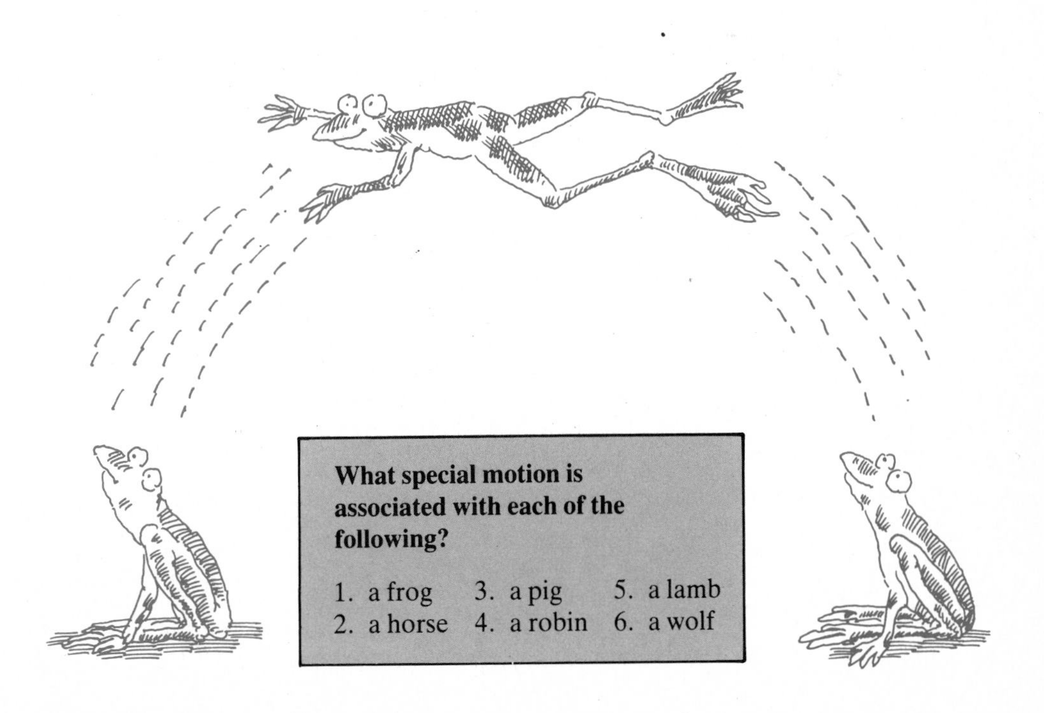

What special motion is associated with each of the following?

1. a frog
2. a horse
3. a pig
4. a robin
5. a lamb
6. a wolf

multiple choice tests

One way of testing your understanding of the meaning of a piece of writing is to give you, say, four or five statements about it or four or five answers to a question about it and ask you to choose the right one.

A multiple choice question about the Migration of the Salmon (above, under *links**) might be: In what way does the writer contrast the behaviour of the salmon with that of other fish? You might have to choose the right answer from these:

a. They can swim backwards.
b. They swim from the ocean up the river.
c. They do not spend all their life in the place where they were born.
d. They do not stay with their eggs till they are hatched out.

narrative composition

The word *narrative* means 'telling a story'. So narrative poetry is poetry that tells a story, and narrative composition is a composition* that tells a story.

Well-written stories, like any other composition, have an introductory paragraph to set the scene, a separate paragraph for each event in the development of the plot* and a final paragraph to bring the plot to a conclusive ending or to reveal the outcome of the events related. It will help you to understand the construction of a story if you ask yourself these questions about the story opposite:

1. In what way does the first paragraph introduce the story?
2. In what way does the last paragraph bring the story to a decisive ending?
3. What events or developments of the story do the second and third paragraphs deal with?

4. How are the paragraphs connected by means of link* words?

The Tables Turned

Alec liked playing practical jokes whenever he could. As soon as he heard that the circus was coming to town, he wanted to play another.

When he saw the circus elephant, he made up his mind what to do. He went to the cake shop and bought the biggest bun he could see. Then he ran home, sliced it open, scooped out the middle and filled it with half a jar of mustard and the contents of the pepper pot.

Having put the bun together again, he went to the circus at feeding time, along with a lot of other people. When the elephant put the bun into its mouth with its trunk, a look of astonishment spread over the huge animal's face, and it coughed and squealed quite loudly.

Alec roared his head off. He was laughing so much that he did not see the elephant suck up a trunkful of water. Alec was doubled up with laughter, and offered an easy target as the elephant directed a massive jet of water down his neck. Alec was soaked – but the crowd was delighted, and the elephant looked very pleased with himself!

negative

A negative is any word or sentence that says no. To reply in the negative means, in effect, to say no. It is the opposite of the affirmative*. A negative sentence is one that contains or implies *not*, eg: These are not my shoes. They will never (that is, *not* ever) fit me!

neuter gender

There is no real neuter gender in English, though it may be said to survive in the pronouns *it* and *its* which refer to things that are neither male nor female.

nicknames

The word 'nickname' comes from 'an eke name', where *eke* means also. A nickname is therefore an 'also-name', an additional name by which a person is familiarly known. Probably everyone knows someone with red hair who is referred to as Ginger, or a fat child called Tubby.

There is usually a good reason for a nickname that sticks. For instance, William Cody was a famous hunter and scout in the days when the Red Indians were trying to stop the pioneers settling in America. It is not difficult to understand how he came to be called Buffalo Bill.

Sometimes a nickname starts as a joke. Little John in the Tales of Robin Hood, you may remember, got his nickname in this way. He was so big and tall that Robin Hood thought it would be a good joke to call him Little John. In the same way a tall boy today is often called Shorty.

Many nicknames are traditional. An Irishman abroad tends to be called Paddy, an Welshman Taffy and a Scotsman Jock. A Briton in Australia is called 'Pommy'. A Murphy is sometimes called Spuds, a Clark Knobby, a Smith Smuts, a Bell Daisy. But other nicknames may be quite original and derive from some special event connected with the person.

noises

Most creatures, and sometimes objects, make sounds. Sometimes the sound is so distinctive that it is given a special name. An ape is said to gibber; a bee drones. There are some more examples in the boxes on this page.

Noises Made by Animals
a bull bellows
a cat purrs
a cow moos
a dog barks
a donkey brays
an elephant trumpets
a horse neighs
a hound bays
a lamb bleats
a lion roars
a monkey chatters
a mouse squeaks

Noises Made by Objects
the beat of a drum
the blare of a trumpet
the rattle of dishes
the report of a rifle
the rustle of leaves
the screech of brakes
the shrill of a whistle
the clatter of hoofs
the clink of a coin
the crack of a whip
the hiss of steam
the jangling of chains
the popping of corks
the skirl of bagpipes

Do you know what these do?	
1. a frog	4. a cock
2. a pig	5. a duck
3. a snake	6. a turkey

nominative case

When the noun or its equivalent is the subject* of the verb, its case* is said to be nominative.

nonsense verse

Any poem that is fun to read but does not make real sense is called nonsense verse. It was made popular by Edward Lear, who wrote this one:

> Far and few, far and few
>   Are the lands where the Jumblies live;
> Their heads are green, and their hands are blue,
>   And they went to sea in a sieve.

Perhaps the most famous nonsense poem is *Jabberwocky*, from *Through the Looking-Glass* by Lewis Carroll, of which this is the first verse:

> 'Twas brillig, and the slithy toves
> Did gyre and gimble in the wabe;
> All mimsy were the borogoves,
> And the mome raths outgrabe.

noun

The names of creatures, things, qualities and ideas are called nouns. The words *man, frog, table, stickiness, truth* are all nouns. Nouns may be divided into proper*, common*, abstract* and collective* types.

noun clause

A group of words containing a main verb* and functioning as a noun, that is, as the subject or object of the sentence, is called a noun clause.

Did you know *that he had won*? (object)
How he won is a mystery. (subject)

novel

A long story published as a complete book is called a novel. These are examples:

Robinson Crusoe by Daniel Defoe
David Copperfield by Charles Dickens
The Borrowers by Mary Norton
The Eggbox Brontosaurus by Michael Denton

number

The form taken by words to show whether they are singular* or plural* is called their number.

numbers

Numbers can be written down in figures, ie arabic numerals* (1, 2, 3 . . .) or roman numerals* (I, II, III . . .), or words. Words should normally be used for numbers below 100 (except in lists of numbers), and at the beginning of a sentence; otherwise you may use figures. See also cardinal numbers*, ordinal numbers*.

obituary

A notice of someone's death, usually in a newspaper, is called an obituary. It most often takes the form of an advertisement inserted by relatives, simply stating the bare facts of who has died, where, and when, and who survives the deceased. But if the person was famous, the newspaper may print a whole paragraph or complete article about the life of the person who has died.

object

The noun* or its equivalent that indicates the creature, thing, quality or idea affected by or receiving the action of a verb* is called the object of the verb. It can be thought of as the answer to the question Whom? or What?

He carried the *child* on his back. (Whom?)
A florist sells *flowers*. (What?)
I like *him*. (Whom?)
She praised his *bravery*. (What?)
He likes *skiing*. (What?)

When the action affects someone or something indirectly, the object is called an indirect object. It is often accompanied by *to* or *for*, as in: I handed the note to *him*. The object is the *note*, and the indirect object *him*. It is still the indirect object when not accompanied by *to*, as in: I handed *him* the note.

objective case

This is the case* of a word that is the object* of a verb or follows a preposition*. It is sometimes called the accusative case. Both the italicized words in these sentences are in the objective case: John kicked the *ball* hard. She put the blame on *him*.

occupations

A person is called different things according to what he is doing. A man is called a father when he looks after his children, a motorist when he drives a car, a pianist when he plays the piano, a liar when he tells a lie, a hero when he does something brave, a footballer when he plays football, and so on. Here are more examples:

An ambassador represents his country abroad.

An angler goes fishing with a rod and line.

An auctioneer sells goods to the highest bidder.

A caddie carries a golfer's kit.

A captor has captured someone.

A cashier takes charge of money.

A chauffeur drives a car for his employer.

Do you know what these people do? Try to match each name with the most appropriate description. If in doubt, consult a dictionary*.

1. A cobbler	plays a flute
2. A confectioner	sells flowers
3. A curator	betrays his country or friends
4. A dramatist	pretends to be someone else
5. A drover	mends shoes
6. A fiddler	has charge of a museum
7. A flautist	writes plays
8. A florist	sells sweets
9. A gaoler	drives cattle or sheep to market
10. A glazier	has charge of a gaol (jail)
11. A groom	plays a fiddle (violin)
12. An impostor	makes furniture
13. A joiner	looks after horses
14. A mason	puts glass in windows
15. A traitor	builds with stone

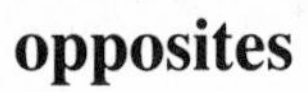

opposites

Words of opposite meaning are called opposites or antonyms*.

ordinal numbers

These are the numbers that show order or position, such as first, sixth, or twenty-third. It is important to know the spelling and abbreviations of ordinal numbers as they are in constant use.

1st first	11th eleventh	21st twenty-first	101st hundred and first
2nd second	12th twelfth	22nd twenty-second	105th hundred and fifth
3rd third	13th thirteenth	23rd twenty-third	260th two hundred and sixtieth
4th fourth	14th fourteenth	24th twenty-fourth	302nd three hundred and second
5th fifth	15th fifteenth	25th twenty-fifth	500th five hundredth
6th sixth	16th sixteenth	26th twenty-sixth	574th five hundred and seventy-fourth
7th seventh	17th seventeenth	27th twenty-seventh	1000th thousandth
8th eighth	18th eighteenth	28th twenty-eighth	
9th ninth	19th nineteenth	29th twenty-ninth	
10th tenth	20th twentieth	30th thirtieth	

origin of words See *derivation**

overworked words

Being a little lazy, we all tend to use the first word or cliché* that comes to us instead of searching for a more exact word. Consequently we use hackneyed* words like *get, nice, awful, great, smashing* too often. They serve well enough in conversation, but in writing, when you have time to pause and choose the best word, you can avoid their vagueness. Instead of saying that an idea is *great*, you should try to say exactly why you approve of it. Perhaps it was helpful, kind, unusual, ingenious, flattering, convincing, indisputable . . .

palindromes

A word or sentence that reads the same backwards as forwards is called a palindrome, eg kayak, madam, minim.

Able was I ere I saw Elba.
Madam I'm Adam.

paragraphs

In a composition*, a group of sentences all dealing with the same topic or stage of development is called a paragraph. We indicate each new paragraph by beginning it a little in from the margin. This is known as indenting. In typing or printing, new paragraphs are sometimes indicated by leaving a line space instead.

Dividing a composition into paragraphs helps the reader to see its stage-by-stage development at a glance. Each paragraph should stick to the one topic or stage and not allow anything else to creep in. Then, to show the progression from one stage to the next, each paragraph should be connected to the one before with a clear link*.

Very often it is wise to indicate in one sentence what the main point of the paragraph is. This may come at the beginning as an introduction, or it may come at the end by way of summing up. In either case it is called the topic sentence*.

parenthesis

Parenthetic words, phrases or sentences are those that are not really part of the sentence or paragraph but just inserted as a comment or to make things clear. The parenthesis may be shown by brackets*.

The next day (fortunately a holiday) it was fine.

It may also be cut off from the rest of the sentence by means of commas* or dashes*.

The last swimmer, by no means the worst, was a boy from Manchester.

Diana was furious – you can hardly blame her – when she discovered that her clothes had gone.

participles

These are the parts of the verb that, with the help of auxiliary verbs*, can be used to form various tenses*. The present participle* always ends with -ing.

I am not *lending* you my clothes.

The past participle* usually ends in -ed, though some 200 verbs are irregular*.

I have *swum* all the morning.

The champion was unexpectedly *beaten*.

Participles can also be used as adjectives*.

The *leading* swimmer.

He was a *beaten* man.

parts of speech

Words may be divided into classes according to the work they do in the sentence. These are called the eight parts of speech: nouns*, verbs*, pronouns*, adjectives*, adverbs*, conjunctions*, prepositions*, interjections*. This jingle may help you to remember which is which:

> Nouns are the names of everything,
> Like *width* or *wisdom, child* or *swing*.
> Adjectives tell about the noun,
> Like *great, small, lovely, rich* or *brown*.
> Instead of nouns the pronouns stand:
> *He* for John, *she* for Ann, *it* for hand.
> Verbs express action, such as *run*,
> *Will read, is building* or *has done*.
> How things are done the adverbs tell,
> Like *slowly, quickly, badly, well*.
> Conjunctions join the words together,
> Like boys *and* girls, wool *or* leather.
> The preposition stands before
> The noun, as *at* or *through* the door.
> The interjections you exclaim,
> Like *Ugh!* it smells, or *Oh!* he's vain.

passive voice

When the subject of the verb has the action done to it, the verb is said to be in the passive voice (the opposite of active voice*). It is mostly used when it is not important or possible, or perhaps wise, to say who did the action:

Derek was taught a lesson.
He was beaten by Diana.

past participle

This is one of the two participles*, and may be used to form tenses* with the help of auxiliary verbs*.

I have not *seen* him for a long while.
He had never *swum* so far in his life.

Participles are often used as adjectives:

She threw the *crumpled* towel away.

They may also be used to join sentences:

He was tired by the exercise. He soon fell asleep.
= Tired by the exercise, he soon fell asleep.

past tense

The form of the verb used to express an action that happened in the past is called the past tense. There are several kinds of past tense:

Past perfect: He had finished tea when I called.
Past continuous: He was watching TV when I called.
Present perfect: He has finished eating.
Past simple: He watched a good programme yesterday.

These are criminals	
accomplice	murderer
burglar	perjurer
blackmailer	pirate
crook	poacher
embezzler	robber
forger	smuggler
kidnapper	swindler
thief	

Do you know what these are?

1. a braggart
2. a spinster
3. a prophet
4. a farrier
5. a pedestrian
6. a tyrant
7. an emigrant
8. an impostor
9. an eavesdropper

people

People are called different names according to the role they are playing (eg their occupation*), or the way someone regards them. You may be seen as a pupil one moment, and as a footballer the next. You could as quickly change to being a cousin, a neighbour, a watcher, a glutton, an optimist, a bully or even an angel. The usual way to define people is like this:

An ancestor is a person from whom you are descended.
A bachelor is an unmarried man.
A conscript is a person compelled by law to serve in the armed forces.
A cynic is a person who sneers at goodness and never believes it to be genuine.
An immigrant is a person who enters your country to settle there.

person

Person is the form the pronoun* takes to indicate whether it refers to the person speaking, called the first person (I, me, we, us); the person spoken to, called the second person (you); or the person spoken about, called the third person (he, she, it, him, her, they, them). Notice that there must be agreement between the verb and the person.

Person	Singular	Plural
First	I try	We try
Second	You try	You try
Third	He tries She tries It tries	They try

personal letters

Letters written to friends or relatives are called personal letters in contrast to business letters*. Their purpose is to keep in touch with friends and cultivate their friendship and to keep on good terms with people you know less well. If you know your friends well you will greet them with their first name or even their nickname*. If they are adults whom you know less well, you will greet them with 'Dear Mrs Brown, Dear Dr Jennings,' etc.

The normal way of ending is 'Yours sincerely', but if you are writing to a close friend you may wish to show this by ending with 'Yours' or 'Yours ever', or 'Your friend'. Another way of ending, especially with relatives, is 'Love', or 'With love from'.

To those you know well you will sign the letter with your first name only, or even perhaps your nickname (if you have one). To those you know less well it is usual to sign with your surname too, eg Jennifer Watkins, Martin Johnson.

Notice how a personal letter is set out. Each new topic requires a fresh paragraph*, just as in other compositions. There is an example on the next page.

32 Angela Lane
Keighley
Yorks
4th June 1984

Dear Diana

Isn't it wonderful! Mum's at last agreed to let me go on holiday with Steve and the Joneses. I can't wait.

We're going in August so, as soon as we break up, can you spend a day shopping with me? I need new shorts, new jeans, a sun-dress and a nice bikini. It's bound to be sunny. Heaven knows how I'll get the money. I'll have to start saving.

Tell John that Steve wants to borrow his Swiss army knife and his guitar, and do congratulate him on winning.

Write soon and tell me all your news.

Lots of love
Liz

Outline of a Personal Letter

1. Address of sender
2. Date written
3. Greeting (salutation)
4. Body of letter
5. Ending or farewell
6. Signature

phonetics

The symbols showing how words are pronounced are called phonetics. Each sound is always represented by the same symbol, regardless of the spelling of the word. For instance, the sound of *c* in *cat* is represented by the symbol k, but so is the *ch* in *chord*. The sound of *sh* in *shirt* is represented by a symbol like an S, but so is the *ti* in *patient*. When we say that a word is spelt phonetically, we mean that it is spelt as it is spoken. *Peep*, for example, is spelt phonetically, but *people* is not.

phrasal verbs

These are the very common verbs that have a little word (sometimes two) attached to them, such as: blow up, try on, give away, bring down, think over, switch off, come in, go up to, get out of. The little word, making it a phrasal verb, often gives the verb a quite different meaning. Notice that its object* can come before or after the little word, though it usually comes after if it is long and always comes before it if it is a pronoun, eg

He thought *the problem* over.
He thought over *all that had happened.*
He thought *it* over.

I GIVE UP.

phrases

A phrase is a group of words often introduced by a preposition, but containing no main verb*. A group of words introduced by a participle*, a gerund* or an infinitive* may also be called a phrase. It may function as an adjective* and tell us about a noun*. In this sentence it tells us about the noun *boy*:

The boy *with the bandaged hand* is my friend Paddy. (preposition)

Or it may function as an adverb and tell us about a verb. Here it tells us about the verb *raced*:

Derek raced *across the bridge* and disappeared. (preposition)

Going into the shop, I bumped into Derek. (participle)

Or it may function as a noun*.

Eating peas with a knife requires skill. (gerund)

To become the champion was his ambition. (infinitive)

pitch

The pitch of a sound is its degree of depth or shrillness. The rise and fall of the pitch of the voice is called intonation*.

plot

The plot is the sequence of events in a short story, novel or play, which forms the outline of the action. Thus every narrative* has a plot and its success as a narrative will depend on its plot, though there are many other factors, such as character drawing, atmosphere, description, and moral values, that make a story good or bad.

plural

The form that words take to show that they mean more than one is called plural, as opposed to singular meaning only one. In English, only nouns*, pronouns* and verbs* (not, for example, adjectives*) have number* (a different form for singular and plural). The singular and plural forms of pronouns are:

Singular	I	you	he	she	it	me	him	her	it
Plural	we	you	they	they	they	us	them	them	them

Some examples of singular and plural verbs are:

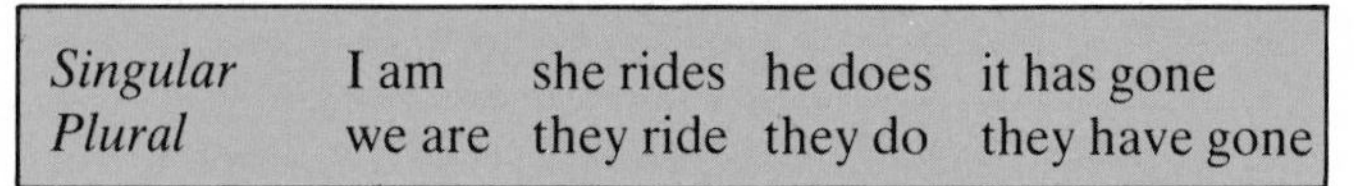

Singular	I am	she rides	he does	it has gone
Plural	we are	they ride	they do	they have gone

The rules for forming the plural of nouns are as follows:

1. Normally the plural is formed by adding -s to the singular: boy – boys, table – tables, nose – noses.
2. But nouns ending in a hissing consonant (s, sh, ch, x, z) add -es: bus – buses, bush – bushes, match – matches, box – boxes, fez – fezes.
3. Those ending in -y with a consonant before it change the y into i and add -es: lady – ladies, city – cities.
4. But those with a vowel before the y simply add -s:

valley – valleys, day – days, toy – toys.

5. Some nouns ending in a single f change the f into v and add -es: leaf – leaves, wolf – wolves. But some may just add -s: chiefs, hoofs, roofs. If the noun ends in -fe, the f is changed to v and -s is added: wife – wives, knife – knives.
6. Most familiar words ending in -o add -es: potatoes, tomatoes, heroes, cargoes, echoes. But these just add -s: pianos, solos, banjos, Eskimos, sopranos, curios, dynamos, magnetos, manifestos.
7. Several nouns have no singular: shears, shorts, pincers, pliers, breeches, scissors, pants, jeans.
8. A few nouns are the same in the plural as in the singular: sheep, deer, salmon, aircraft, cod.
9. A few are irregular*: tooth – teeth, mouse – mice, foot – feet, child – children, man – men, ox – oxen, woman – women, goose – geese.

What are the plurals of these?

1. patch
2. shelf
3. berry
4. elbow
5. donkey
6. fly
7. curio
8. policeman
9. glass

poetry

Poetry is writing in verse* form, which is always rhythmical and sometimes rhymed. In serious poetry (as opposed to joke poems*), the language used is more concentrated, more finely expressed and more moving than prose*. Here is an example of rhymed verse from William Wordsworth's *Daffodils*:

> I wandered lonely as a cloud
>   That floats on high o'er vales and hills,
> When all at once I saw a crowd,
>   A host, of golden daffodils;
> Beside the lake, beneath the trees,
>   Fluttering and dancing in the breeze.

These unrhymed lines from Tennyson's *Ulysses* are moving too, in another way:

> The lights begin to twinkle from the rocks;
> The long day wanes; the slow moon climbs; the deep
> Moans round with many voices. Come, my friends,
> 'Tis not too late to seek a newer world.
> Push off, and sitting well in order smite
> The sounding furrows; for my purpose holds
> To sail beyond the sunset, and the baths
> Of all the western stars, until I die.

possessive adjectives

The possessive adjectives are: my, your, his, her, its (no apostrophe*), our, their. They are used to point out which, eg my foot, your books, its paw, our country, their car.

possessive case

The form of the noun or pronoun used to show possession is called the possessive or genitive* case. Possessive nouns show their case by means of the apostrophe*. They add *'s* to the singular noun, eg John's mother, his friend's house, Tess's nose. If the plural ends in *s*, the possessive noun simply adds an apostrophe, eg those girls' clothes, the thieves' getaway. But if the plural does not end in *s*, it adds *'s*, eg the policemen's uniforms, the children's toys.

possessive pronouns

The possessive pronouns (mine, yours, his, hers, its, ours, theirs) should not be confused with the possessive adjectives*. Possessive pronouns stand instead of a possessive adjective and a noun*: That calculator is *mine* (my calculator).

Is that the Kitsons' dog? Yes, it is *theirs* (their dog).

postcards

Plain postcards are used for sending brief messages that do not contain anything really private – such as an acknowledgment of receiving something, instructions to tradesmen, or reminders about sports fixtures. Picture postcards have a picture on one side and a brief message (often from a holiday) and the address on the other. There is no need to write a greeting*, and the writer's address may be omitted or shortened if it is already known, or if no reply is expected.

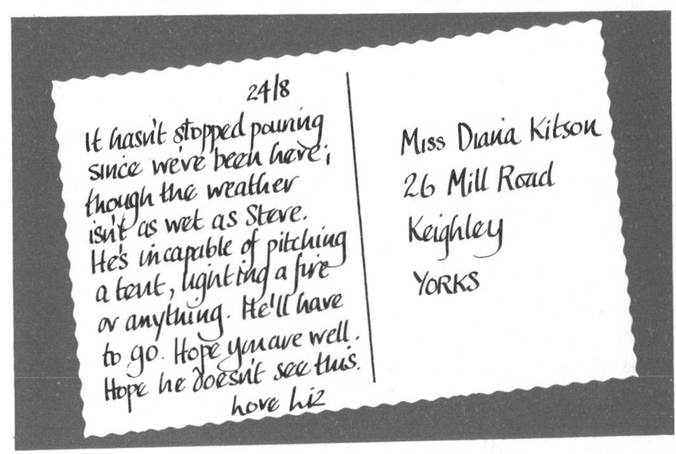

24/8

It hasn't stopped pouring since we've been here; though the weather isn't as wet as Steve. He's incapable of pitching a tent, lighting a fire or anything. He'll have to go. Hope you are well. Hope he doesn't see this.

Love Liz

Miss Diana Kitson
26 Mill Road
Keighley
YORKS

précis

This is the name for a short, continuous piece of writing which gives a summary of all the main points in a longer piece of writing.

predicate

The part of the sentence that tells us about the subject* is called the predicate. It always contains the main verb. In these sentences the predicates have been italicized:

Dogs *bark*.
This little boy *is surprisingly heavy*.
Mr Jones *rushed suddenly round the corner*.
Suddenly round the corner rushed Mr Jones.

prefixes

A prefix is a syllable or little word placed before a root word to modify its meaning and so build a new word. Very many words in English have prefixes. Most of them were already added when the words were borrowed, but some prefixes are still used to form new words today. Some recent words formed with prefixes are: *mini*skirt, *super*man, *uni*sex, *tele*vision, *pro*-American, *anti*-American, *ex*-wife, *counter*productive, *co*partnership.

Most prefixes come from Old English, Latin or Greek. Here are examples of some of the more common ones:

Old English Prefixes

a- (meaning on) aboard, afloat, align, aloft, ashore
be- (to make) becalm, befoul, befriend, begrimed, belittle
fore- (before) forebear, forebode, forecast, forehead, foretell
mis- (wrong) misapply, misappropriate, mischance, misdeed, misplace
off- (from) offload, offputting, offset, offshoot, offspring
out- (beyond) outbid, outdistance, outlaw, outlive, outrun, outvie
over- (over) overcook, overdo, overhead, overreach, overrule, overseer
un- (not) uncommon, uncouth, undated, unflappable, unleavened
un- (reverse) unbend, unclench, uncoil, uncouple, undone, unhinge, unravel
with- (back) withdraw, withhold

Latin Prefixes

ab- (away from) abdicated, abduct, aberration, abnormal, abstract
ad- (to) adhere, adjective, adjunct, adjust, adventure, adverb
ante- (before) antedate, antediluvian, antenatal, anteroom
bene- (well) benediction, benefactor, benefit, benevolent
bi-, bis- (twice) biceps, bicycle, bifocal, bigamy, biscuit, bisect
circum- (around) circumference, circumnavigate, circumstances
co- (with) coeducation, co-operation, co-opt, copartnership

counter- (against) counteract, counter-attack, counterfoil
de- (down, away) depend, depose, descend, detach, dethrone, detract
dis- (negative) disappear, discourage, disgraceful, disown, dissimilar
ex- (out of) excavate, exclude, exhale, expatriate, expel, export
in- (not) inaccurate, inanimate, inaudible, incredible, insipid
in- (into) inbred, incision, inclusive, induction, inhale, inject
inter- (between) interact, intercede, interlude, intermediate, interval
non- (not) non-combatant, non-conformist, nondescript, nonentity, nonsense
ob- (against) object, obscure, obstacle, obstinate, obstruction
per- (through) perambulate, perceive, percolate, perforate, pervade
post- (after) postdate, postgraduate, post-mortem, postpone, postscript
pre- (before) precede, predestination, predict, prefix, prehistoric
pro- (before) proceed, procure, progress, project, prologue, prospect
re- (again) reappear, recreate, reflect, reformed, repeat, retreat
semi- (half) semicircle, semicolon, semi-detached, semi-final, semi-tropical
sub- (under) subcontract, subheading, subhuman, submarine, subnormal
super- (above) superfluous, superhuman, supernatural, supersonic, supervisor
trans- (across) transatlantic, transfer, transit, transmission, transport
tri- (three) triangle, tricolour, tricycle, trilogy, tripod
ultra- (beyond) ultramarine, ultra-modern, ultrasonic, ultra-violet
uni- (one) unicorn, uniform, unisex, unison, universal
vice- (in place of) vice-admiral, vice-captain, viceroy, viscount

Greek Prefixes

anti- (against) anti-aircraft, antibiotic, antibody, anti-semitic, anti-social
arch- (chief) archangel, archbishop, archduke, arch-enemy, arch-knave
auto- (self) autobiography, autograph, automatic, automobile, autonomous
homo- (same) homoeopathy, homogeneous, homonym, homosexual
hyper- (over) hyperbole, hypercritical, hypermarket, hypersensitive
mono- (single) monocle, monogamy, monologue, monoplane, monopoly, monotone
poly- (many) polyanthus, polygamous, polygon, polytechnic
tele- (from afar) telegram, telepathy, telephone, telescope, televise

prepositions

These are little words used to introduce phrases*. The most common ones are: in, on, into, at, from, by, beside, alongside, to, under, with, through, over, above, like, within, after, before, upon, along, behind, towards, below, inside, of, up, down, about, for.

Sometimes two or three words may act as one preposition. Examples of these compound prepositions are: on to (*not* onto), out of, up to, as regards, with regard to, in front of, in respect of.

In standard English, you should never use a preposition to end a sentence *with*. Sentences like that last one can usually be turned around to avoid this, for example: Never end a sentence with a preposition.

In the following sentences the phrases have been enclosed in brackets and the prepositions italicized.

The girl (*in* the Rolls Royce) was (*on* TV) last night.

Teresa saw that her friend was (*in* great danger) and ran (*like* the wind) (*to* her rescue).

Paddy took (*with* him) a net (*for* catching tadpoles).

Prepositions make phrases with nouns or their equivalent. Because it comes before a noun or its equivalent, we say that the preposition governs it, and that the noun or its equivalent is in the objective case*. You can see this best in the last example, where *him* is governed by the preposition *with*, since *him* is the objective form of *he*.

present participle

The present participle is the part of the verb ending in *-ing* used to form certain tenses* with the help of auxiliary verbs, eg I am *working*; she was *reading*; he has been *running*.

Participles* may also be used as adjectives*, eg the *steaming* kettle; *coming* events; *yapping* dogs.

present tense

This is the tense* usually used to express a state of affairs that exists or an action that takes place in the present or has a habit of happening. There are two main forms in English. The present continuous shows an action as going on now: They are playing football. It is raining.

The present simple is used for making general statements or to express an action that has a habit of happening:

The earth moves round the sun.
He loves criticising people.
She has a lot of friends.
He knows all the answers.
John is the best player I know.

pronouns

These are the words used instead of nouns to avoid the awkwardness of having to keep repeating them, eg:

When Mrs Jones had dived into the water, Mrs Jones shouted out that the water felt much warmer than the water felt last time Mrs Jones had swum in the water.

This sounds much less clumsy when written with the help of pronouns:

When Mrs Jones had dived into the water, *she* shouted out that *it* felt much warmer than *it* felt the last time *she* had swum in *it*.

Pronouns may be divided into five kinds: personal pronouns*, relative pronouns*, possessive pronouns*, interrogative pronouns*, demonstrative pronouns*.

Personal pronouns*: I, you, he, she, it, we, they, me, him, her, us, them.

Relative pronouns*: who, whose, whom, which, that.

Possessive pronouns*: mine, yours, his, hers, its, ours, theirs.

Interrogative pronouns*: what, who, which, whom, whose.

Demonstrative pronouns*: this, these, that, those, the other, others, such, the same.

Some proper nouns with their adjectives	
America	American
Arab	Arabic
Australia	Australian
Barbados	Barbadian
Belgium	Belgian
Buddha	Buddhist
Christ	Christian
Canada	Canadian
China	Chinese
Cyprus	Cypriot
Denmark	Danish
Egypt	Egyptian
Finland	Finnish
France	French
Ghana	Ghanaian
Greece	Greek
Guiana	Guianese
Holland	Dutch
Iran	Iranian
Iraq	Iraqi
Ireland	Irish
Isle of Man	Manx
Israel	Israeli
Italy	Italian
Jamaica	Jamaican
Japan	Japanese
Jew	Jewish
Malaya	Malay
Mexico	Mexican
Norway	Norwegian
Portugal	Portuguese
Sweden	Swedish
Spain	Spanish
Switzerland	Swiss
Turkey	Turkish
Venice	Venetian
Vienna	Viennese
Wales	Welsh

proper adjectives

These are adjectives* formed from proper nouns*, eg *British* is formed from the proper noun *Britain*, *Victorian* is formed from *Victoria*, and *Pakistani* is formed from *Pakistan*. Because proper nouns all begin with a capital letter, proper adjectives also begin with a capital letter. They mostly end with -ish or -an, but there are many exceptions.

proper nouns

These are nouns that name particular persons or things, and they always begin with a capital letter to distinguish them from common nouns*. Thus the common noun *river* names any river, but the noun *Amazon* names one particular river and is therefore a proper noun.

Proper nouns may name individual people (Joan, Mr Smith), animals (Spot), countries (Indonesia), counties (Yorkshire), towns (Dundee), streets (High Street), lakes (Lake Nyasa), oceans (Pacific), buildings (The White House), boats (Wayfarer), days (Saturday), months (February), companies (Marks and Spencer), religions (Hinduism), organisations (The Royal Society for the Prevention of Cruelty to Animals), or languages (Hebrew).

prose

Any ordinary continuous writing that is not written according to a system of rhyme or rhythm is called prose, to contrast it with verse*.

Try turning any rhyming poem that you know into prose.

proverbs

A short wise saying that has been used by many people for a long time is called a proverb. Proverbs may contain advice (Make hay while the sun shines), a warning (Listeners hear no good of themselves), or simply wisdom (Necessity is the mother of invention).

A wise saying is unlikely to become a proverb unless it is easy to remember. Consequently proverbs are always neatly worded and to the point. Many are cleverly balanced (More haste, less speed). Some are rhymed (Birds of a feather flock together).

Proverbs have a deeper meaning than the obvious literal one; they are figurative*. It is true that the farmer should make his hay while the sun shines. But as a proverb the saying is not necessarily meant in that literal sense. It is used figuratively to suggest that we should take advantage of an opportunity while it is available. If, for instance, friends invited you to spend a holiday in their home on the Mediterranean, and you hesitated to accept the invitation, your mother might advise you to make hay while the sun shines, because the opportunity for such a holiday might never arise again.

Some Popular Proverbs
A stitch in time saves nine.
New brooms sweep clean.
Half a loaf is better than no bread.
Least said, soonest mended.
Don't put all your eggs in one basket.
A rolling stone gathers no moss.
He who pays the piper calls the tune.
A bird in the hand is worth two in the bush.
As you make your bed, so you must lie on it.
Actions speak louder than words.
Beggars cannot be choosers.
Don't change horses in mid-stream.

punctuation

The main punctuation marks are: full stop*, comma*, question mark*, exclamation mark*, semi-colon*, colon*, apostrophe*, inverted commas*, dash*, brackets*. The sole purpose of punctuation marks is to make reading matter easier to follow and prevent ambiguity*. Without punctuation, for instance, it would be difficult to show the difference between these two sentences:

I don't believe that John cried.
'I don't believe that!' John cried.

puns

A pun may be defined as a humorous play upon words that have a similar sound but different meanings. Some are based on homonyms*, eg

Is life worth living?
It depends upon the liver.

Here the play is upon *liver*, which can mean either a part of the body or someone who lives. The humour lies in the ambiguity* – in not knowing which is meant. Many puns depend upon homophones*, eg

They went out and told the Sexton,
And the Sexton tolled the bell.

Here the play is upon *told* and *tolled*, which sound alike. It's funny spoken aloud because you don't know which is meant. In print this kind of pun is less effective, since it's given away by the spelling.

Many people groan when they hear puns, to express approval or disapproval. But they shouldn't disapprove of them, because it takes a lively mind to make them up.

question marks

The question mark (?) is placed at the end of sentences to show that a direct question is being asked, but it is not used after an indirect or reported question, eg

What are you doing, Steve?
I asked Steve what he was doing.

When a direct question is written as a quotation, the question mark is placed inside the quotation marks, as in:

'What are you doing, Steve?' I asked.

questions

A sentence takes an interrogative or question form when it asks for information. A direct question is always accompanied by a question mark*, but the indirect question has no question mark because the question is indicated by the wording.

quotation marks

This is another name for inverted commas*. As well as indicating the exact words of a speaker, they are used in handwritten prose where italics would be used in printer's type, to indicate titles of books, slang, words picked out as words, words not meant literally, or short quotations, eg

'Robinson Crusoe' was written by Daniel Defoe.
I told him to 'keep his hair on'.
The word 'tantalize' has an interesting origin.
When he complained that she had paid too much for the dress, she reminded him that 'a thing of beauty is a joy for ever'.

quotations

Any repetition of words previously spoken or written is called a quotation. When a quotation from a book, poem or article runs to several lines, it usually stands on its own. If it is just a few words, it is made part of the sentence and enclosed in quotation marks*.

recipes

Instructions for preparing and cooking food are called recipes. These instructions need to be very clear so that the cook will not make a mistake and spoil the food. The recipe usually begins by listing the ingredients needed. The instructions that follow take the form of a series of commands telling you exactly what to do at each stage. Here is the recipe for making 3 or 4 portions of chocolate pudding:

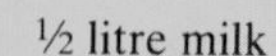

½ litre milk
3 rounded tablespoons of chocolate powder
100 grams of breadcrumbs
1 tablespoon sugar
1 egg
½ teaspoon vanilla

Mix the chocolate powder and milk in a small saucepan. Stir over gentle heat until well blended. Add the breadcrumbs and sugar and cook for two minutes. Remove from heat, and place the pan in a bowl of cold water for a minute. Add the egg and vanilla. Beat vigorously with a rotary or wire whisk. Pour the mixture into a well-buttered soufflé dish or pudding basin, cover with buttered paper, and place in the oven. Bake at Gas No 3 for about 30–40 minutes. Take it out and try pressing gently with a finger – if it springs back, it's ready.

When cooked, turn pudding out on to a dish. Serve hot or cold, with cream or custard.

reference books

Any book to which you refer for particular information may be called a reference book. You refer to a dictionary* for the meaning of words; to a book of street maps to find a road; to an atlas to find a country, river, mountain or city; to a telephone directory to find a telephone number; to a catalogue to find the description and price of goods for sale, and to an encyclopedia for information about almost anything.

All these are reference books and all rely on alphabetical order* to help you find the information. Where the information is arranged in some other (eg geographical or chronological) order, you will always find an alphabetically arranged index* at the end.

Do you know what you will find in these reference books: an almanac, a flora, a thesaurus, a gazetteer, a lexicon?

reflexive pronouns

These pronouns show that the action expressed by the verb is reflected back on the doer of the action, so that the object* is the same as the subject*. They are: myself, yourself, himself, herself, itself, ourselves, yourselves, themselves, oneself.

He has cut *himself* on a piece of glass.
She could have kicked *herself* for breaking the bottle.
They pride *themselves* on their carefulness.
I thought to *myself* that there would be trouble.

Reflexive pronouns can also be used as emphatic pronouns*.

relative pronouns

The relative pronouns are: who*, whom, whose, that, which, where. They connect adjective clauses* to the rest of the sentence. They also serve to join two sentences together.

This is the house. Jack built it.
= This is the house *that* Jack built.

I have lost the pen. Gary gave me it.
= I have lost the pen *which* Gary gave me.

We met a boy. He had lost his dog.
=We met a boy *who* had lost his dog.

This is the farmer. I drove his tractor.
= This is the farmer *whose* tractor I drove.

Ann spoke of a girl. Do you know her?
= Do you know the girl of *whom* Ann spoke?

We visited the factory. These sweets are made there.
= We visited the factory *where* these sweets are made.

The relative pronoun should be placed as near as possible to the noun to which it relates. If it gets out of place you end up saying some very funny things, such as: We at last found the dog near the little girl that had the curly tail.

reported speech

This is another name for indirect speech*.

requests

The kind of command* that is worded very politely is called a request. Requests are usually written with a question mark, since they are really commands expressed as questions to make them polite. It is as well to know how to make polite requests, if you want to get people to do things for you!

rhymes

An exact similarity of sound between the last syllables* of words from the last accented vowel onwards, is called a rhyme. Thus *hung* rhymes with *wrung*, and *realize* rhymes with *revise*. But *song* does not rhyme with *hung*, nor does *exclaim* rhyme with *complain*. Notice that in English the spelling of words is no safe guide to whether they rhyme. *Though* does not rhyme with *bough*, but it does rhyme with *sew*.

Can you pair these words off as rhymes?	
1. cow	sum
2. tea	bough
3. case	pun
4. wise	part
5. two	buys
6. earth	bee
7. time	worth
8. heart	face
9. one	who
10. come	rhyme

rhythm

The rhythm of a line of verse depends upon the accent* of the words when spoken aloud. It is often called metre. Each unit of the metre is called a 'foot'; each foot is made up of one or more syllables, one of which is stressed (accented). Here is a common rhythm of Ti-tum (unaccented, accented):

. — . — . — . — . —

And still/they gazed/and still/the won/der grew

. — . — . — . — . —

That one/small head/could car/ry all/he knew.

riddles

A riddle used to mean anything puzzling and mysterious – the riddle of the universe, for example. But today it generally means just a conundrum, a question meant to puzzle and amuse. The humour lies in the unexpected answer. Sometimes this depends on a pun:

> Why is Sunday the strongest day?
> Because all the others are week-days.

A popular type has a pun in the question as well:

> Why did the jam roll?
> Because it saw the kitchen sink.

Some riddles depend on the answer being utterly beside the point:

> Why don't elephants ride bicycles?
> They haven't got thumbs to ring the bell with.

Sometimes their humour depends on a too obvious interpretation of the question:

> Why do we buy shoes?
> Because we can't get them for nothing.

Some riddles depend on the construction of a word:

> Why is SMILES the longest word in the language?
> Because there is a mile between the first letter and the last.

Some make use of a familiar phrase or proverb in an unexpected way:

> Why does a giraffe eat so little?
> Because it makes a little go a long way.
>
> How many ponies can you put in an empty stable?
> Only one, because after that it won't be empty.

But a good many are just clever puzzles:

What is not much use till it is broken?
An egg.

What is it that I can see but you can't?
The back of your head.

What goes up but never comes down?
Your age.

roman numerals

These are figures used by the ancient Romans and still used occasionally today when we need variety. For instance, a book's introductory pages may be numbered with roman numerals to distinguish them from the main text.

The symbols consist of these basic ones and combinations of them, sometimes using small letters: I = 1 V = 5 X = 10 L = 50 C = 100 D = 500 M = 1000

In the combinations you will notice that lower number symbols placed before V, X, L, C and D mean less than, while the same symbols placed after them mean more than. Thus XL means 40 (50−10), while LX means 60 (50+10). Try doing some arithmetic with roman numerals – you won't find it easy! Here are some more roman numerals:

I = 1	XI = 11	XXX = 30	XC = 90	CCCXL = 340
II = 2	XII = 12	XXXII = 32	XCV = 95	CDX = 410
III = 3	XIII = 13	XXXIV = 34	C = 100	D = 500
IV = 4	XIV = 14	XL = 40	CVIII = 108	DCCC = 800
V = 5	XV = 15	L = 50	CX = 110	CM = 900
VI = 6	XVI = 16	LV =55	CXIX = 119	M = 1000
VII = 7	XVII = 17	LX = 60	CXX = 120	MDCCC = 1800
VIII = 8	XVIII = 18	LXVII = 67	CXXX = 130	MCMLII = 1952
IX = 9	XIX = 19	LXX = 70	CXL = 140	MCMLXXXV = 1985
X = 10	XX =20	LXXX = 80	CL = 150	MM = 2000

salutation

This is another name for the greeting* in a letter.

sarcasm

This is a bitter way of speaking that is intended to wound, eg 'I suppose you think you know everything!' Sarcasm often uses irony*.

The equator is a menagerie lion.

schoolboy howlers

Sometimes young people make mistakes that the more 'knowing' find funny. These have been labelled schoolboy howlers. Many of them were real mistakes originally, but others have been invented by grown-ups to make people laugh. You can often tell which are the invented ones as they tend to be far-fetched, like the last example below.

The horizon is the place where the earth and sky meet but disappear when you get there.

Moths do not need much food because they eat holes.

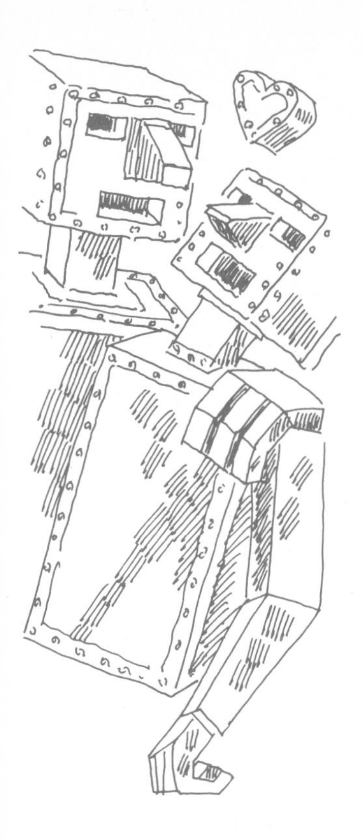

scientific language

Modern science uses a very technical vocabulary derived mainly from Greek and Latin, with words such as bacteria, electron, supersonic, uranium or photoelectric. The language in which scientific matters are described has to be as free as it can be from human emotions and prejudices. Experiments, for example, are usually reported impersonally and often use the passive*, eg

The temperature was raised to 100° and then the bar was transferred to its new position.

second person

This is the form the pronoun takes when it refers to the person spoken to: *you*. There used to be a separate second person singular (thee/thou), but it is no longer in common use. The other kinds of person* are first person* and third person*.

semi-colons

The main use of this punctuation mark (;) is to join two parts of a sentence that would otherwise be joined by a conjunction*.

We mustn't dawdle; it is very late. (because)
It is quite tame; it never runs away. (and)

sentence adverbs

Unlike ordinary adverbs, sentence adverbs do not tell us about a verb only, but about the whole sentence. They are, so to speak, inserted in the whole sentence and, to show this, they are marked off from the rest of the sentence by commas. There are some examples on the next page.

Sardines are little fish that swim into tins, lock themselves up and leave the key outside.

Nevertheless, the money must be found. When we looked for it, *however*, we could not find it anywhere. *As a matter of fact*, no one really believed that it had been stolen. Perhaps it was a false alarm, *after all*.
Other common sentence adverbs are:
for example, in the meantime, even so, please, thank you, yes, no, indeed, for instance, therefore, in this way, in a sense, in fact.

sentences

A complete thought expressed in words is said to be a sentence. A sentence normally has a subject* and a predicate*. It is written with a capital letter at the beginning and it may end with a full stop*, a question mark* or an exclamation mark*.

Sentences may be classified as statements*, questions*, commands*, requests* or exclamations*.

When you build a sentence, the unit is the word. When you build a composition, however, the unit is the sentence. They come in all varieties and sizes: long sentences or short ones, inverted sentences, sentences in indirect* or direct speech*, literal* sentences or figurative* sentences. Using different kinds of sentence to express exactly what you have to say is what makes a good composition.

short answers

The natural, and therefore best, answer to some questions is a short one, using Yes or No on their own or with an auxiliary*. The full answer is understood, as in:

> Is this the money you found?
> Yes. *or* Yes, it is.
> (Yes, it is the money I found.)

shorthand

This is a system of rapid writing by hand, using signs to represent sounds or groups of sounds. It is especially helpful to reporters who cannot write down what is said in longhand as quickly as it is spoken. The shorthand system most widely used in Britain is Pitman's.

This says:
NOW IS THE TIME FOR ALL GOOD MEN TO COME TO THE AID OF THE PARTY.

sick jokes

Sick humour is about things that have a darker or crueller side to them. Although these cruel things are not in themselves funny, these jokes shock people into laughing in a 'sick' way. In this joke it is the husband's amazing indifference to his wife's suffering that is implied.

> 'Doctor, it is very urgent,' said the voice at the other end of the line. 'My wife swallowed my black ballpoint two hours ago.'
> 'Why didn't you phone me sooner?' asked the doctor.
> 'Well, I have been using my red ballpoint since, but it has just run out.'

silent letters

In English we have certain letters that appear in the spelling of words but are not sounded in speaking them. In some cases the silent letter once had a sound, but for one reason or another people have ceased to pronounce it. The letter has remained in the spelling, which shows that English spelling has not changed much for a couple of centuries.

We also have a silent e in words like love, give, have, above because formerly there was only one sign for u and v. To indicate that the consonant v was intended and not the vowel u, a silent e was attached for the consonant.

Some Words With Silent Letters
hearse (a)
scent (c)
handsome (d)
solve (e)
gnaw (g)
caught (gh)
ghostly (h)
comb (b)
knowledge (k)
calm (l)
autumn (n)
island (s)
thistle (t)
biscuit (u)
wrestling (w)

similar words

The technical name for words of similar meaning is synonyms*. Words that look the same are called homonyms*, and words that sound the same are called homophones*.

similes

We often compare one thing with another because it is similar in some particular way though quite different in every other respect. Thus we may say that Steve is *as proud as a peacock* or that he struts about *like a peacock.* In comparing him with a peacock we are emphasizing his pride. We mean that he is very proud. This figurative* use of language is known as a simile. If we said that Steve was like his father, it would not be a simile but just a literal comparison.

There are dozens of stock similes, all worth knowing; but if you use them without thought, they tend to become stale and can be regarded as clichés* (expressions to be avoided in careful writing). To make your writing fresh and interesting, you should try to create your own similes and make your descriptions vivid in your own way, as the poet did who described a becalmed ship with the simile, 'as idle as a painted ship upon a painted ocean'.

Can you complete these traditional similes?
1. as agile as a —
2. as alike as ——
3. as blind as a —
4. as clean as a —
5. as easy as —
6. as — as a fiddle
7. as — as a dove
8. as — as a hunter
9. as — as a lamb
10. as — as the grave

singular

This form of words indicates that only one is referred to – as opposed to plural*, which refers to more than one. Singular and plural are known as number*. In English only nouns* (bush – bushes), pronouns* (he – they) and verbs* (am – are) have number, not, for example, adjectives*.

slang

Words and phrases used in everyday intimate conversation but not used in polite or serious conversation are called slang, eg round the bend, son of a bitch, keep your hair on, a smashing time, that snooty bird, to come a purler, the fuzz, browned off.

In 1912 words like *bogus, boom, rollicking, rowdy* were still considered slang, but they are part of standard English today. Many of our words and idioms* began as slang and gradually became acceptable as polite English. It is almost certain that some of the slang in use today will in years to come be accepted in the same way. In the meantime, whatever is considered slang should be avoided in your compositions unless put in inverted commas to show that you know it is slang, or put into the mouth of a speaker who would use slang when speaking.

small ads

Small ads are plain advertisements in newspapers or magazines inserted by individuals rather than firms. They come under headings like: Wanted, For Sale, Appointments, Situations Vacant, Lost and Found, Domestic Help Wanted, Used Cars, Services Offered.

They are sometimes referred to as Classified Advertisements. They are usually brief because advertisers are charged according to the number of words or lines.

SERVICES

HABIT BREAKERS – The stop smoking course used by top companies. Want to stop smoking but can't? Call John on 041 2329.

UNATTACHED? Liz Ash marriage friendship bureau. Send SAE 32 Angela Lane, Keighley, Yorks.

CV'S Professionally compiled and presented £1.50 × age. Details: 321-1314.

speeches

To make a speech sound like a delivered speech rather than a formal composition, you add little personal touches such as: 'I will give you an example', 'Let me tell you why', or 'I will explain'.

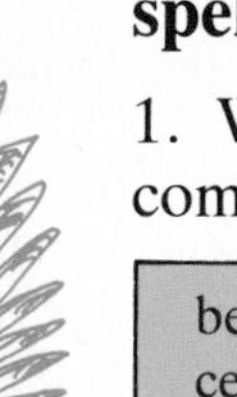

spelling rules

1. When a word has a sound like *ee* in *meet*, *i* comes before *e*, except after *c*:

belief, field, pier, chief, siege ceiling, receive, deceit, conceivable *exceptions*: seize, weird, counterfeit, Keith

2. When you add a suffix* to a word ending in *y*, you change the *y* into *ie* or *i* only when a consonant* comes before it.

tidy – tidies – tidied – tidily *but* volley – volleys – volleyed – volleying berry – berries, *but* monkey – monkeys *exceptions*: You keep (or even add) a *y* when adding -ing to avoid a double i, eg tidy – tidying, cry – crying, tie – tying (*but* ski – skiing).

3. When you add a suffix to words ending in a single *e*, you drop the *e* when the suffix begins with a vowel*.

nose – nosing – nosed – nosy, *but* noseless care – caring – cared, *but* careful – careless retire – retiring – retired, *but* retirement *exceptions*: If a soft c or g comes before the e, the e must be kept to keep the c or g soft, eg notice – noticeable, courage – courageous. Other exceptions are: true – truly, due – duly, awe – awful; shoe – shoeing, hoe – hoeing, toe – toeing.

4. When you add a suffix beginning with a vowel to a one syllable* word ending with a vowel and a consonant, you double the consonant.

fit – fitting – fitted – fitter – fittest *but* fitness, fitful, fitly star – starry – starring – starred *but* starlit, starless, starlet *exceptions:* bus – buses, gas – gases

5. In words of more than one syllable ending in a single consonant with a single vowel before it, you double the consonant only if the last syllable is accented*.

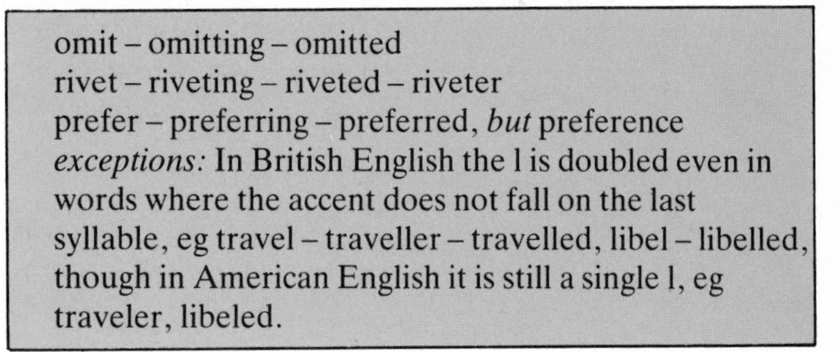
omit – omitting – omitted
rivet – riveting – riveted – riveter
prefer – preferring – preferred, *but* preference
exceptions: In British English the l is doubled even in words where the accent does not fall on the last syllable, eg travel – traveller – travelled, libel – libelled, though in American English it is still a single l, eg traveler, libeled.

6. When you add *-ly* to words ending in *-le*, you drop the *-le*.

able – ably, gentle – gently, wobble – wobbly

7. Verbs ending in c add k when adding *-ed, -ing, -y* or *-er*, in order to keep the c hard.

mimic – mimicked, bivouac – bivouacking, panic – panicky, picnic – picnicker

8. A few words ending in double l, like *full, till, well, all,* lose an l when used to form compound words*.

full – careful, till – until, well – welcome, all – altogether

9. The verbs *advise, devise, license, practise*, and *prophesy* all take c in their noun form:

good advice, a clever device, your licence, regular practice, a true prophecy.

10. For the spelling of the plural form of nouns, see plurals*.

spoonerisms

An accidental changing over of sounds between two words, producing a funny result, is called a spoonerism. The name comes from a certain Dr Spooner, an academic at Oxford who was always mixing things up. For example, he once started a hymn, 'Kinkering congs their tatels tike', when he meant 'Conquering kings their titles take'. What was meant by these spoonerisms?

No, I was sewn into this sheet.
A half warmed fish entered his mind.

stage directions

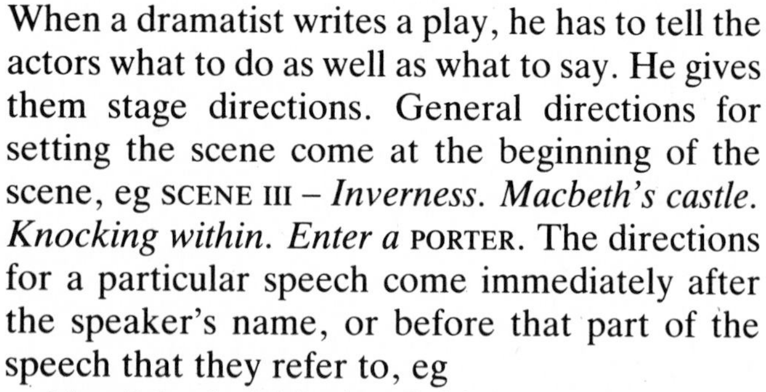

When a dramatist writes a play, he has to tell the actors what to do as well as what to say. He gives them stage directions. General directions for setting the scene come at the beginning of the scene, eg SCENE III – *Inverness. Macbeth's castle. Knocking within. Enter a* PORTER. The directions for a particular speech come immediately after the speaker's name, or before that part of the speech that they refer to, eg

Mrs Otherly (rising): I think I will go.
Lincoln: Think kindly of me. (*He takes her hand.*) Goodbye, Mary.

Other directions, for actions not associated with speeches, go on a separate line at the point where the action is due to happen, as with Shakespeare's famous line:

Exit, pursued by a bear.

standard English

The kind of English that is acceptable to most educated people is called standard English. It is more easily recognized in written English than in spoken, since the way people speak depends upon where they were brought up. A Glaswegian's rendering of standard English will sound quite different from a Londoner's.

statements

When a sentence* simply gives information, states a fact or gives a reply, it is called a statement. A sentence that does not ask a question, give an order or exclaim something is a statement. Every statement begins with a capital letter and ends with a full stop and, if it shows the actual words spoken, it is punctuated with inverted commas*.

There is little or no rain in a desert.
'I have to do some shopping,' he said.

stories

Stories are narrative compositions*. A long story filling a whole book is called a novel*. A short story teaching a lesson and usually having animals as characters is called a fable*.

subject

The part of a sentence* that tells us who or what 'does' the action of the verb* is called the subject. The other part of the sentence, the part that tells us about the action in all its detail, is called the predicate*. In these sentences the subject has been italicized. The rest of the sentence is the predicate.

The boy stood on the burning deck.
The girl in the pretty dress is going to sing.
Where are *my shoes*?
What a wonderful player *that boy* is!
(*You*) Fetch some water, please.

suffixes

Something added to the end of a word to make a new word is called a suffix. For example, the suffix *-ly* added to *bad* makes *badly* and *-ance* added to *assist* makes *assistance.* An understanding of the use of suffixes will enable you to build thousands of words. These are the main ones:

-able (capable of being; used to form adjectives* from verbs*) distinguishable, agreeable, desirable, enjoyable, movable

-al (an adjective ending) fatal, ironical, medical, musical, plural, tidal, verbal

-age (to form abstract nouns*) drainage, breakage, leakage, patronage, marriage, stoppage

-an (forms adjectives meaning belonging to) American, European, Trojan, urban, surburban

-ance (to form abstract nouns from verbs) appearance, deliverance, ignorance, guidance, perseverance

-ant (a person who does something) accountant, assistant, descendant, inhabitant, servant

-ar (to make adjectives meaning like something) angular, circular, globular, insular, linear, nuclear

-ary (to form adjectives meaning of a certain sort, or for a certain purpose) cautionary, legendary, military, primary, secondary, revolutionary

-ate (to form verbs, especially those meaning to make into) duplicate, consolidate, invalidate, liquidate, necessitate, tabulate

---

-dom (to make abstract nouns meaning the condition of) boredom, freedom, martyrdom, serfdom, wisdom

---

-ee (denoting persons) absentee, addressee, employee, payee, refugee, referee, trainee

-en (to form verbs meaning to make) broaden, darken, enliven, fatten, harden, quicken, slacken, thicken

-ence (to form abstract nouns from verbs) coincidence, difference, excellence, existence, preference

-er (to form nouns meaning a person or thing that does something) blackmailer, boiler, builder, follower, singer, sniper, steamer
-er (to form the comparative* of adjectives) cheaper, dearer, flatter, greater, hotter, leaner, thinner, wiser
-ess (to denote a female) actress, countess, duchess, goddess, lioness, tigress
-est (to form the superlative* of adjectives) cheapest, dearest, fastest, latest, meanest, nicest, rowdiest

---

-fold (times) fourfold, hundredfold, manifold, sixfold
-ful (to make adjectives meaning 'full of' from nouns) cheerful, doubtful, harmful, joyful, shameful, spiteful, successful
-fy (to form verbs meaning to make, to make into) amplify, classify, falsify, magnify, purify, simplify, terrify

---

-ible (to make adjectives meaning capable of being) collapsible, exhaustible, irrestistible, perfectible
-ing (to make the present participle* or gerund*) acting, beaming, cracking, fearing, gazing, joking, meddling, wobbling
-ion (to make abstract nouns) adhesion, attention, decision, division, opinion, relegation, temptation
-ise (an ending for certain verbs) advertise, chastise, despise, disguise, exercise, supervise, surprise
-ish (to make adjectives meaning like something, or to qualify another adjective) boyish, childish, foolish, largish, lightish
-ism (to make abstract nouns denoting a theory or system) criticism, capitalism, idealism, mysticism, socialism, spiritualism
-ist (to make nouns denoting someone who believes or practises something) atheist, botanist, chemist, florist, idealist, realist, specialist
-ity (to make nouns denoting the quality of what the adjective describes) absurdity, formality, equality, finality, reality, scarcity, vivacity
-ive (to make adjectives meaning 'tending to' from verbs) active, aggressive, explosive, impressive, offensive, possessive
-ize (to form verbs from nouns or adjectives) equalize, idolize, materialize, naturalize, patronize, realize, vaporize

---

-less (to make adjectives meaning without) countless, endless, graceless, nameless, pointless, shapeless

-like (to make adjectives meaning like) godlike, kinglike, lifelike, warlike, workmanlike

-ly (to make adverbs* from adjectives) beautifully, cruelly, dutifully, guilelessly, merrily, quickly

---

-ment (to make abstract nouns denoting state or action) arrangement, engagement, improvement, payment, retirement, settlement

---

-ness (to make abstract nouns denoting state or condition) bitterness, blindness, goodness, loudness, rudeness, stoutness, thickness

---

-or (to form nouns denoting agent or doer) donor, editor, governor, incubator, sponsor, surveyor, tailor, tractor

---

-ship (to make abstract nouns denoting the quality of being this or that) fellowship, friendship, hardship, ownership, membership, scholarship

-some (to make adjectives meaning apt to or apt to be) awesome, irksome, lonesome, quarrelsome, tiresome, wholesome

---

-th (to make abstract nouns from verbs and adjectives) dearth, growth, length, health, stealth, strength, wealth, width

---

-wise (to make adverbs of manner) anticlockwise, contrariwise, lengthwise, likewise, otherwise, slantwise

---

-y (to make adjectives from nouns) dirty, earthy, messy, misty, thorny, sulky, stony

---

Try your hand at word building. Use each of these suffixes once to make a word from one of the words below.

-ful	-ible	-able	-atic	-en	-ive
-some	-ment	-ism	-ness	-ar	-ish

1. line	5. system	9. notice
2. disdain	6. thin	10. hero
3. collapse	7. bereave	11. girl
4. length	8. quarrel	12. object

superlative

The superlative form of the adjective* or adverb* expresses the highest degree in any comparison. The superlative of adjectives is usually formed by adding -est to the adjective:

tall – tallest, fine – finest, angry – angriest

But with longer adjectives the superlative is formed by using *most*:

beautiful – most beautiful, awkward – most awkward

And a few adjectives are irregular:

good – best, bad – worst, far – farthest *or* furthest

A few short adverbs form their superlative with *-est*:

late – latest, soon – soonest

But usually adverbs form their superlatives by means of *most*:

John worked *most tidily*.

You have to finish the *most rapidly* to win.

A few adverbs are irregular:

well – best, badly – worst

THE TALLEST

THE BEST

THE WORST

THE MOST IRREGULAR

surnames

In early times people had just one name that was given them at birth, their personal name. One name was quite enough at first. If someone mentioned Hilda or John, everyone knew who was meant because there would be only one Hilda and one John in a tiny village. But as time went on, tiny villages grew into big villages or even towns. Then there might be several Johns and several Hildas living in the same place. How were people to know which John or which Hilda was meant?

In order to distinguish one person from another with the same name, there grew up the habit of adding a byname or short description of the person, such as John the small man, John the carpenter, John from Ross, John up the hill, John son of William. These bynames belonged to the one person only and died with their owner. They were rather like our modern nicknames*.

Gradually for various reasons some of these bynames were passed on to sons. For instance, when John the carpenter died it would be quite natural for his son Tom to be called Tom the carpenter, since sons in those days nearly always followed their father's trade. At any rate, in time bynames were inherited by the family and became surnames as we know them today. The bynames mentioned above became Smallman, Carpenter, Ross, Hill and Williamson (William's son).

By 1400 most people in England had surnames. They came a little later in Scotland, Wales and Ireland. Before long they were so firmly established as family names, regardless of what the family happened to be doing or where it was living, that John Carpenter could well be a baker and William Baker a carpenter.

There were a number of different types of bynames from which surnames derived. There was the kind that distinguished a man by his appearance or character, eg Tom the long fellow or Tom the bright man. These gave rise to surnames such as Short, Brown, Small, Longman, Longfellow, White, Trueman, Goodman, Brightman, Coward.

Perhaps most surnames of all have come from bynames distinguishing a man by his trade, eg Stephen the miller or Stephen the butler. These gave rise to names such as Baker, Barber, Brewer, Butcher, Carter, Chandler, Cook, Falconer, Dyer, Farmer, Fisher, Forester and Glover.

Then there were those bynames that showed where people had come from, eg George from York, or George from Holloway. These account for surnames such as Bolton, Clifton, Crosby, Dudley, Kirby, Sutton and Wells.

Other bynames showed where in the neighbourhood the person lived, and gave rise to surnames such as Brook, Castle, Field, Green, Grove, Heath, Hill, Holt or Lake.

Finally, many surnames came from bynames that distinguished a man by his father, eg Robertson (Robert's son), Nixon (Nick's son) Johnson (John's son), Robinson (Robin's son). In Scotland and Ireland the word for *son* was *Mac*, giving rise to names such as McDonald (son of Donald) and McAllister (son of Allister). In Ireland the old word for a descendant was abbreviated to O', giving rise to names such as O'Reilly (son of Reilly) and O'Doherty (son of Doherty).

In early times the smith, the man who made things from metal, was a very important person. The word is used for goldsmiths, blacksmiths, tinsmiths and coppersmiths, and it has left behind it the most common surname of all – Smith.

Another medieval occupation that has produced an unusually high number of surnames is that of the wright. The name means maker. The maker of carts was called a cart-wright, the maker of wheels a wheel-wright and the maker of ships a ship-wright. This is why we have so many names like Wright, Wainwright, Cartwright.

Surnames such as these are easy to trace back to their beginnings, but the origin of others is much less certain. Hook and Crook might originally have been bynames attached to a fisherman and a shepherd. On the other hand, both words once meant a bend in a river. It is thus possible that John Hook and Peter Crook may both be descended from men who centuries ago lived by the bend of a river.

But supposing your surname is Bugle; did your first ancestor with the name play a bugle, or did a large clump of the flower called bugle grow outside his house?

And what about the surname of Overandover from Nottingham? Did his ancestor bore everyone by telling his stories over and over, or could he have been an acrobat famous for his somersaults?

Can you think what the origin of each of these surnames was?

1. Noble	6. Townsend
2. Tyler	7. Fairchild
3. Hastings	8. Anderson
4. Meadows	9. Thomson
5. Cornwall	10. Naylor

Can you find synonyms for these words?

1. wrath
2. miserable
3. annually
4. bravery
5. quickly
6. consume
7. occasionally
8. feeble
9. sturdy
10. vanish
11. scared
12. meagre
13. wealthy
14. velocity
15. vacant

syllables

A sound made with a single effort of the voice, separately from the sounds before or after it, is called a syllable. A syllable must contain one vowel* sound, and it may contain one or more consonant* sounds. The vowel sound may be spelt with more than one vowel letter. The following words are divided into syllables:

day dai-ly fool-ish-ly excit-ing-ly
pho-tog-raph-er syn-on-y-mous-ly

synonyms

Words that have the same or similar meaning are called synonyms. Thus *little* and *small* are synonyms, and so are *try* and *endeavour*.

There are many synonyms in English, but their meanings are rarely exactly alike. Even when they seem to be alike, we usually find that they are alike only in certain contexts*. *Little*, for example, means exactly the same as *small* in these sentences:

His bedroom was a *small* room at the rear.

His bedroom was a *little* room at the rear.

Yet you could not use *small* instead of *little* in this sentence:

A *little* care would have prevented the accident.

Synonyms are rarely interchangeable; usually we have to choose the right word for the particular situation.

Synonyms always beong to the same part of speech*: synonyms of nouns* are nouns and synonyms of adjectives* are adjectives:

brightness, brilliance (nouns)
bright, brilliant (adjectives)
brightly, brilliantly (adverbs)
brighten, enliven (verbs)

Some Useful Synonyms

abbreviate – shorten
abode – dwelling
abrupt – sudden
abundant – plentiful
adversity – misfortune
altitude – height
amiable – friendly
ample – plentiful
animosity – hatred
annual – yearly
apparel – clothes
apparition – ghost
arrogant – haughty
assembly – gathering
assistance – aid
astonishment – amazement
attired – dressed
avaricious – greedy

beverage – drink
brief – short

catastrophe – disaster
cautious – careful
cease – stop
celebrated – famous
centre – middle
chivalrous – gallant
circular – round
colossal – huge
commence – begin
compel – force
comprehend – understand
conceal – hide
conclusion – ending
conversation – talk
courage – bravery
courageous – brave
courteous – polite
cunning – sly
custom – habit

deceive – misguide
difficult – hard
diligence – perseverance
dusk – twilight

edible – eatable
elude – escape
eminent – famous
encircle – surround
enemy – foe
energetic – active
enormous – huge
extend – enlarge
exterior – outside

famous – noted
fatigue – weariness
ferocious – fierce

glamorous – charming
gleam – shine
gorgeous – splendid
grateful – thankful
grave – serious
grip – grasp

indolent – lazy
insane – mad
insolent – cheeky
intention – purpose
interior – inside
intoxicated – drunk
invincible – unbeatable

jovial – jolly
just – fair

loathe – hate
lubricate – oil

matrimony – marriage

maximum – most
minimum – least
moisture – dampness
mute – dumb

noisy – rowdy

obstinate – stubborn
odour – smell
option – choice

penetrate – pierce
persuade – coax
portion – part
procure – obtain
profit – gain
prohibit – forbid
purloin – steal
putrid – rotten

rarely – seldom
recollect – remember
retreat – withdraw
roam – wander

sever – separate
slender – slim
squander – waste
stern – strict
sufficient – enough
surrender – yield
suspend – hang

test – try
tranquil – peaceful

unite – join

vanquish – defeat

tall stories

Any statement or narrative* that is so exaggerated or unlikely that it is hard to believe may in general be called a tall story. It was developed into a literary form by Baron Munchhausen, whose funny stories such as this one became very popular and are still retold today.

My name, as all the world knows, is Baron Munchhausen. I want to tell you about one of my exploits. It happened during the siege of Gibraltar. I sailed to the rock to see my old friend General Elliot, who was in command of the garrison.

I had brought with me a most excellent telescope. By the aid of this instrument I discovered that the enemy was about to discharge a thirty-six pound shell at the very spot where we stood. I told the general about my discovery. He too looked through the telescope and found that my calculation was right.

With his permission I at once ordered a forty-eight pounder to be brought to the spot. I continued to watch the enemy till I saw the match placed at the touch-hole of his cannon. At that very instant I gave the signal for our gun to be fired too.

About midway between the two cannons, the shells struck each other with amazing force. The effect was staggering. The enemy's shell was driven back with such force that it killed the man who fired it, and then knocked out sixteen more enemy as it travelled on. It was still travelling so fast that it crossed the Straits on its way to the coast of Africa. Here its force, after passing through the masts of three enemy ships lying in the harbour, was so much spent that it only just broke its way through the roof of a poor man's cottage, where it damaged a few teeth belonging to an old woman lying asleep on her back with her mouth open. The cannon ball lodged in her throat, but otherwise she was quite unhurt.

Meanwhile, our cannon ball also did quite good service. For it not only drove back the enemy's in the way I have described. It went on its way as I intended it should. It hit the very cannon that had just been fired against us and forced it into the hold of the ship. There it fell with so much power that it broke through the bottom of the ship. This caused the ship to fill and sink immediately. It went down with a thousand Spanish sailors on board, besides many soldiers.

This, to be sure, was a most extraordinary exploit. I will not, however, take all the credit myself. My judgment was indeed the chief cause of its success, but chance also helped me a little. For I found out afterwards that the soldier who charged our forty-eight pounder had put in, by mistake, a double quantity of powder.

technical terms

Any words and phrases to do with a particular art, skill or science may be called technical terms.

Words such as *synonyms** or *auxiliary verbs** could be considered technical terms belonging to the study of language*, while *sonata* and *tonic key* are technical terms from music, and *crystalline thermoplastics* and *thermoforming composites* are technical terms from chemistry.

tenses

The form of a verb* which helps to indicate when the action took place is called its tense. Present tense*, future tense*, and past tense* are the main divisions of tense.

thank-you letters

This term covers any letter written to show your gratitude, whether for a present, a party, a holiday, a special treat, or a good turn. Your thanks should be warm without being overdone if you wish to sound sincere.

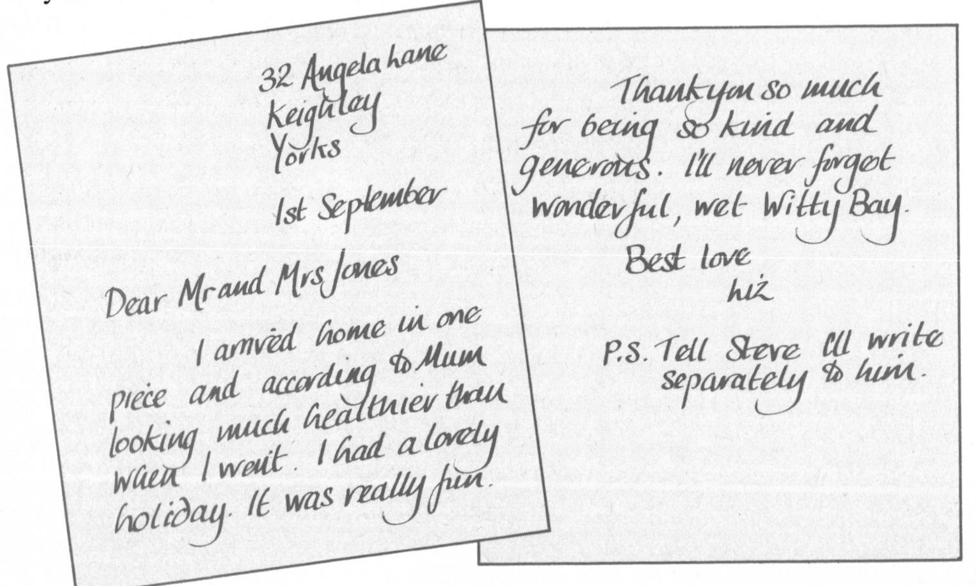

32 Angela Lane
Keighley
Yorks

1st September

Dear Mr and Mrs Jones

I arrived home in one piece and according to Mum looking much healthier than when I went. I had a lovely holiday. It was really fun.

Thank you so much for being so kind and generous. I'll never forget wonderful, wet Witty Bay.

Best love
Liz

P.S. Tell Steve I'll write separately to him.

third person

The pronoun* takes this form when it refers to the person or persons spoken about. The third person pronouns are: he, him, his, she, her, hers, it, its, they, them, theirs, himself, herself, itself, and themselves. Notice that the form of the verb* also changes with person*. We say *I am*, but *he is*; *you try*, but *she tries*.

times

Usually times are written down in figures (3.00 3.30 3.45 12 o'clock). If there is any doubt as to whether the morning or afternoon is meant we add *am* or *pm* (3.00 am 3.30 pm 12.00 noon 12.00 midnight). If we are using the 24-hour clock, as is usual in international timetables, there is no need for any addition to the figures (03.00 15.30 12.00 24.00).

But it is also useful to know how times are spoken or written down in words:

three o'clock in the morning
three-thirty in the afternoon
half past three in the afternoon
twelve o'clock noon, *or* midday
twelve o'clock at night, *or* midnight

With the 24-hour clock, times are sometimes spoken differently, for example: three o'clock, twelve noon, *but* fifteen-thirty (15.30), sixteen hundred hours (16.00).

titles

The title of a book, play, or film is usually printed in italics*. When it is handwritten it may be underlined or put in inverted commas*. The main words of the title are usually begun with a capital letter, like these:

The Origin of Species
Look Back in Anger
The Charge of the Light Brigade

tongue-twisters

Any saying that is so difficult to say that it seems to twist the tongue into knots is called a tongue-twister. The trickiness is often caused by the quick repetition of a consonant*, as with this old chestnut:

> Peter Piper picked a peck of pickled pepper;
> a peck of pickled pepper Peter Piper picked.
> If Peter Piper picked a peck of pickled pepper,
> Where's the peck of pickled pepper Peter Piper picked?

A more recent one that is nearly as ridiculous, also depending on repeated consonants, is:

> If you saw a pink pug puppy playing ping-pong with a pig, or a great grey goat a-golfing with a goose, would you think it half as funny as a big brown bunny blowing bubbles with a bishop in a boat?

In this one there is difficulty with vowel* sounds as well as consonants:

> A fly and a flea in a flue
> Were wondering what to do.
> Said the fly, 'Let us flee!'
> Said the flea, 'Let us fly!'
> So they flew through a flaw in the flue!

The above example could be called comic verse*, though it is rather irregular. Some tongue-twisters use more polished comic verse, such as this limerick*:

> A man who was new to the zoo
> Was told to look after the gnu.
> The gnu knew that he was new
> And he knew that the gnu knew;
> Yes, he knew the gnu knew that he knew.

Now try repreating the words 'Red lorry, yellow lorry' a lot of times, very quickly, and see if your tongue doesn't get in a twist!

topic sentence

It helps the reader to see more clearly the full meaning of a paragraph* if one sentence* points to the real essence of it or indicates what the essential topic of it is. Such a sentence is called the topic sentence. It often comes at the beginning of the paragraph, as with this one from Dickens:

> There are very few moments in a man's existence when he experiences so much ludicrous distress, or meets with so little charitable commiseration, as when he is in pursuit of his own hat. A vast deal of coolness and a peculiar degree of judgment are requisite in catching a hat. A man must not be precipitate, or he runs over it. He must not rush into the opposite extreme, or he loses it altogether. The best way is to keep gently up with the object of pursuit, to be wary and cautious, to watch your opportunity well, get gradually before it, then make a rapid dive, seize it by the crown, and stick it firmly on your head: smiling pleasantly all the time as if you thought it as good a joke as anybody else.

Here the topic of the paragraph is the difficulty of catching your hat. Dickens lets us know straight away that this is the topic. His topic sentence comes first, and the rest of the paragraph discusses this topic, and nothing else.

Sometimes the reader is kept in suspense, waiting till the end of the paragraph to be told what it is all about. Here is such a paragraph from A. R. Horne:

> Baffin's Land lies between Greenland and the North of Canada, and it is intensely cold there. No trees are to be found within a thousand miles of it. Yet an explorer discovered, buried beneath the surface of the earth, an immense forest in perfect preservation. The trees were found lying upon their sides just as if they had been blown over in a gale. Even the cones from the tree-tops were as fresh as the day they fell. All this shows that at one time Baffin's Land must have been much warmer than it is now.

Occasionally the topic sentence will come somewhere else in the paragraph. In this short one from R. L. Stevenson it comes in the middle. The main point the writer is making is that he wants to do all the good and kindness he can. He states this in the topic sentence in the middle, giving one reason in the sentence before and another in the sentence after it.

> I expect to pass through this world but once. Any good therefore that I can do, or any kindness that I can show to any fellow-creature, let me do it now. Let me not defer or neglect it, for I shall not pass this way again.

transitive verbs

The word *transitive* comes from the Latin meaning 'going across'. A transitive verb* requires an object* to complete it, the action of the verb 'going across' to the object, as in:

Paddy *kicked* the ball hard.

Here the ball received the action; the kick 'goes across' to the ball.

With intransitive verbs, there is no going across of the action to an object:

The ball *disappeared* into the distance.

Sometimes the same verb can be transitive or intransitive:

The guitarist played a chord.
(transitive)
The guitarist played well.
(intransitive)

twin words

Words that are regularly used together as doubles, sometimes meaning different things but more often just adding a synonym* for emphasis, may be called twin words.

Some Twin Words
beck and call
fast and furious
down and out
far and away
to puff and blow
kith and kin
safe and sound
to rave and rant
under lock and key
over and done with
in fear and trembling
old and grey
to chop and change
hither and thither
to and fro
up and down

verbs

The part of speech* that expresses something happening (went, thought) or being (am) is called a verb. A verb has *tense**, showing when it happened; *person**, showing who is the subject*; *number** (singular* or plural*), showing whether one or more than one is named by the subject, and *voice**, showing whether the verb is active* or passive*. So, for example, 'It will be squashed' is the third person singular future simple passive form of the verb 'squash'.

A verb may have an object* and be transitive*; it may be intransitive, standing on its own without an object (eg I exist); it may be an incomplete verb* with a complement*; it may be a phrasal verb*; it may be made up of one or more auxiliary verbs* and a participle*; it may be irregular*. It is called a main verb when it has a clear subject, as in 'he goes'.

The tenses can be set out like this (these examples are in the active voice):

The present simple tense
I work every day.
You work every day.
He works every day.
We work every day.
You work every day.
They work every day.

The past simple tense
I phoned yesterday.
You phoned yesterday.
She phoned yesterday.
We phoned yesterday.
You both phoned yesterday.
They all phoned yesterday.

The present perfect tense
I have just played.
You have just played.
Tom has just played.
We have just played
You two have just played.
The boys have just played.

The present continuous tense
I am working now.
You are working now.
She is working now.
We are working now.
You are working now.
They are working now.

The past continuous tense
I was phoning at that time.
You were phoning at that time.
He was phoning at that time.
We were phoning at that time.
You were all phoning at that time.
They were both phoning at that time.

The present perfect continuous tense
I have been playing for an hour.
You have been playing for an hour.
Wendy has been playing for an hour.
We have been playing for an hour.
You have been playing for an hour.
They have been playing for an hour.

The future simple tense
I shall/will practise tomorrow.
You will practise tomorrow.
Sarah will practise tomorrow.
We shall/will practise tomorrow.
You will practise tomorrow.
They will practise tomorrow.

The past perfect tense
I had already tidied the room.
You had already tidied the room.
He had already tidied the room.
We had already tidied the room.
You had already tidied the room.
They had already tidied the room.

The future continuous tense
I shall/will be practising then.
You will be practising then.
Steve will be practising then.
We shall/will be practising then.
You will all be practising then.
The girls will be practising then.

The past perfect continuous tense
I had been tidying the room.
You had been tidying the room.
She had been tidying the room.
We had been tidying the room.
You had been tidying the room.
They had been tidying the room.

verbs of saying

When we write dialogue*, we usually state who says the words. The verb that says who is speaking is called the verb of saying. Besides the simple *he said, she replied, I asked*, there are many other verbs of saying, some of which show very clearly the manner in which the speaker spoke.

'Don't come near me!' *screamed* the angry woman.
'How I hate the cold!' *complained* the old lady.
'Give them back to your sister,' *ordered* Mr Lee.
'You have kept me waiting,' *grumbled* Mrs Jones.
'Hard work is the surest way of succeeding in a job,' his father *reminded* him.
'Why did you borrow my bicycle without permission?' John *demanded*.
'Never mind; perhaps it will be fine tomorrow,' *smiled* Mrs Kitson.

verse

The word *verse* originally referred to a line of a certain length, because you turned back (Latin *verto* = turn) and began another before you came to the edge of the paper. Therefore verse, as opposed to prose*, is any composition* written with lines of a certain length that have a more or less regular beat or accent*. Traditionally, each line begins with a capital letter regardless of whether it starts a new sentence. In addition, the lines often rhyme*. Serious verse is usually referred to as poetry*; less serious verse is called comic verse (see joke poems*) or doggerel*.

The other meaning of 'verse' is one of the divisions into which a poem may be broken. Each division or verse may be held together with a rhyme scheme. A verse usually consists of 4, 6 or 8 lines and is sometimes called a stanza. Here are the opening verses of *The Inchcape Rock* by Robert Southey:

> No stir in the air, no stir in the sea,
> The ship was as still as she could be;
> Her sails from heaven received no motion,
> Her keel was steady in the ocean.
>
> Without either sign or sound of their shock,
> The waves flowed over the Inchcape Rock;
> So little they rose, so little they fell,
> They did not move the Inchcape Bell.

vocabulary

The words you can use in speech or writing are called your vocabulary. The words you can understand when you hear them (your passive vocabulary) are much more numerous than those you can use in your own speech or writing (your active vocabulary). It often helps to extend your vocabulary if you make lists of words used for a particular purpose. Here are some words you might collect for describing people:

Figure tall, short, lanky, dwarfish, gangling, curvacious, stout, slim, frail, athletic, muscular, weedy, buxom, well-built, hefty, stooped, sturdy, drooping, robust, skinny, shapely, petite, brawny, manly, powerful, deformed, gigantic

Face and head round, oval, long, square-jawed, thin, fat, puffy, plethoric, rubicund, flat, pear-shaped, wrinkled, wizened, rosy, pale

Nose long, flat, snub, pointed, broad, bulbous, prominent, enormous, turned-up, aquiline, pitted, Roman

Hair curly, wavy, permed, straight, matted, coarse, unkempt, fine, tangled, blond, brunette, grey, silvery, auburn, ginger, mousy, straw-coloured, silky, glistening, plaited

Eyes bright, clear, staring, brown, blue, grey, hazel, sly, merry, beady, shifty, sparkling, twinkling, round, almond-shaped, dull, bloodshot

Skin rough, smooth, freckled, pimply, blotchy, pale, sunburnt, tanned, golden, florid, ruddy, dusky, fair, bronzed, calloused

Voice soft, loud, low, high-pitched, shrill, squeaky, hoarse, deep, firm, harsh, grating, agreeable, rasping, croaking, melodious, husky, raucous, nasal, gutteral, monotonous

Character careful, cautious, steady, upright, impetuous, excitable, rash, bold, timid, shy, assertive, forthcoming, forward, selfish, mean, generous, kind, cruel, helpful, meek, greedy, modest, boastful, diffident, arrogant, cheerful, miserable, bright, gloomy, optimistic, pessimistic, proud, vain, spiteful, sincere, loyal, disloyal, stubborn, obstinate, charming

vogue words

These are words that for a time are used far more often than they ever were before. They are like catchwords* on a slightly more serious level. On becoming fashionable, they are often given a slightly different meaning. In the 1930s vogue words included *feasible, hectic, individual, psychological moment*. More recently, *allergic, chronic, expertise, literally, nostalgic, phenomenal*, and *summit* have been in vogue. In the 1980s fashion has already favoured many words including *ongoing* and *situation*. Can you think of any others?

voice

This is the form of the verb* that shows whether the subject* is performing the action (active voice*), or is on the receiving end of the action (passive voice*), eg

Paddy headed the ball. (active)
The ball was headed by Paddy. (passive)

In the first sentence the subject *Paddy* performs the action; in the second the subject *ball* suffers the action.

vowels

Sounds produced when the breath passes freely through the mouth without obstruction are called vowels. All the other sounds are consonants*. Vowel sounds are represented mainly by the letters a, e, i, o, u and by combinations of them, eg:

th*a*t	sh*o*p	m*ai*n	p*ee*p	p*ie*r
th*e*m	b*u*st	t*au*t	th*ei*r	f*oo*t
h*i*ll	m*ee*t	m*ea*t	p*eo*ple	s*ou*nd

The five letters are often called vowels, though they are better called vowel letters. The letter *y* is used to represent one vowel sound in such words as *fly, my, try, reply*, and another vowel sound in words like *funny, merry, pony, ugly*.

When two vowel sounds glide together to make one sound, they are called a diphthong*.

who and whom

'Who' is the relative pronoun* used to refer to one or more people. *Who* is used for the subject* of the verb* in its clause*, and *whom* is used when the pronoun is the object* of the verb in its clause. 'Steve, *whom* Liz loves, seems quite different from the boy *who* so annoyed her yesterday.'

The case* of the noun* for which the pronoun stands makes no difference: 'Steve' is the subject of 'seems', but 'whom' is in the objective case* because it is the object of 'loves'.

word families

Words are built from existing words mainly by adding prefixes* (un + done = undone), or suffixes* (care + less = careless), and by making compounds* (bed + room = bedroom, long + playing = long-playing). It helps to extend your vocabulary* if you become aware of the whole family of words that can be built from a single word.

Can you make similar lists for these?

1. sand
2. sleep
3. pass
4. grade

grace	appear	cross
graceful	appearance	crossness
gracefulness	apparent	crossly
graceless	apparently	across
disgrace	disappear	uncrossed
disgraceful	disappearance	crosswise
disgracefully	reappear	crossword
gracious	reappearing	cross-country
ungracious	reappearance	cross-examine

word games

Word games that extend your vocabulary* include crosswords*, word squares, making anagrams*, acrostics*, glidograms and word ladders and finding words beginning with a chosen letter for a whole list of things. Here is a glidogram:

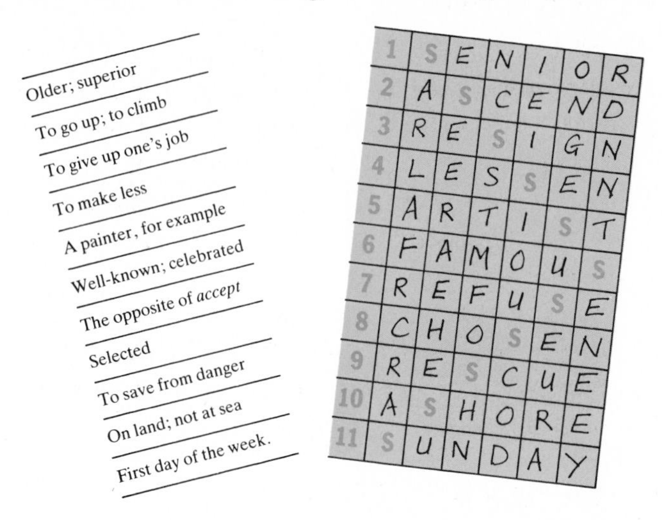

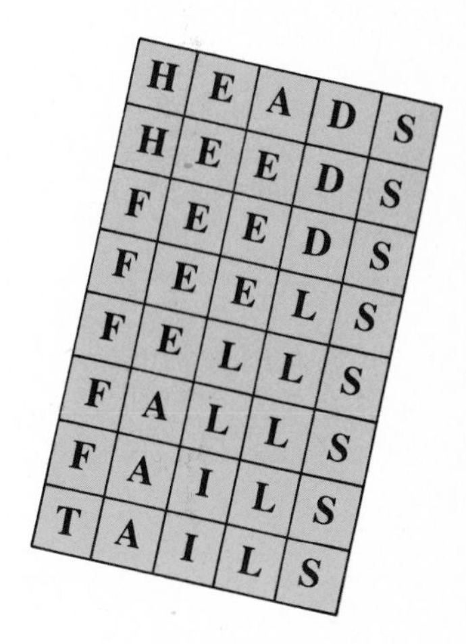

This word ladder changed HEADS into TAILS. Can you change BOAT into SHIP in the same way, one letter at a time, in only five steps?

In the game called hangman, you ask someone to guess a word, letter by letter. Each time they get a letter wrong, you draw one line of a gibbet. If they don't guess the whole word before you've finished, they get hanged!

words with more than one meaning

When an ambiguous* word has two completely different meanings, you can think of it as two different words which happen to have the same spelling. We call them homonyms*. But many words have several related meanings. Some common words have as many as a dozen meanings, for instance, *beat*:

1. to hit or strike
2. to stir vigorously and repeatedly
3. to hammer metal into shape
4. to defeat
5. to perplex; to be too difficult for
6. to thrash as a punishment
7. to throb; to pulsate
8. greatly fatigued; exhausted
9. a regular stroke or sound
10. a pronounced rhythm (of music)
11. referring to those who broke free from convention in the 1960s ('the beat generation')
12. a route regularly patrolled by a policeman

With which meaning is the word *beat* used in each of these sentences?

a. The *beat* of the music was just right for dancing.
b. I am sure we can *beat* them next time we play.
c. Use a plastic whisk to *beat* the eggs.
d. Tony felt dead *beat* after the race.
e. The nurse felt for the *beat* of the pulse.
f. In his anger he *beat* the table with his fists.
g. The problem *beats* me completely; I give up.

"WHERE ON EARTH HAVE YOU BEAN – I MEAN BEEN?"